Tips

▶ Help your child focus on the tasks by minimizing distractions such as television.

▶ Explain directions before your child begins a new type of activity.

▶ Check your child's work and help correct errors. Praise a job well done!

▶ Encourage your child to talk about the work. For example, what did he or she like or not like about the task?

Supplies

▶ scissors

▶ glue stick or glue

▶ crayons or colored pencils

▶ marking pens

▶ pencil

▶ clear tape

Table of Contents

Follow the Bones!

Color the dog bones in order from 0 to 10 to reach the doghouse.

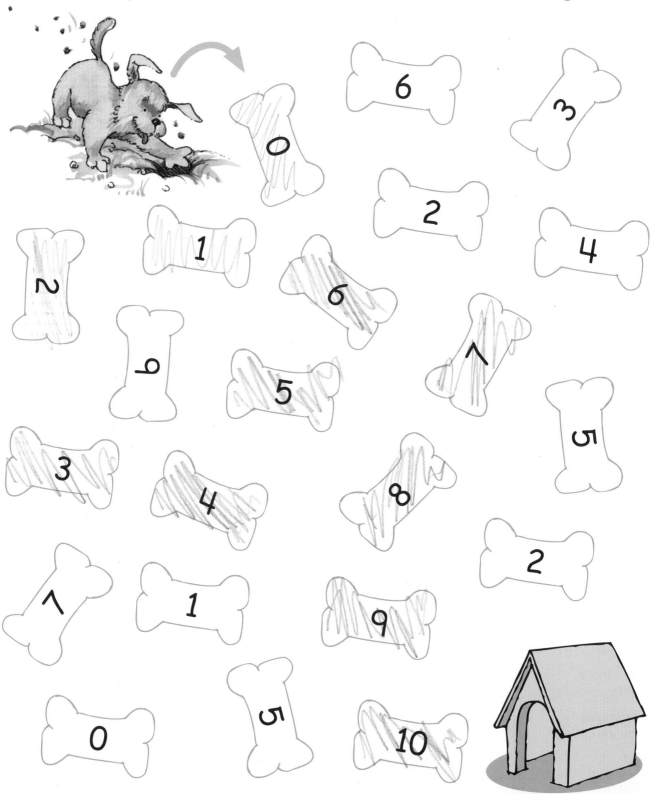

Under the Apple Tree

Read the word on each apple. If the vowel makes the sound you hear at the beginning of apple, color the apple red.

How many red apples are on the tree?

Sailing, Sailing

Trace each letter.

A A A   a a a

C C C   c c c

E E E   e e e

I I I   i i i

Color the picture.

Aa = red   Cc = blue   Ee = purple   Ii = yellow

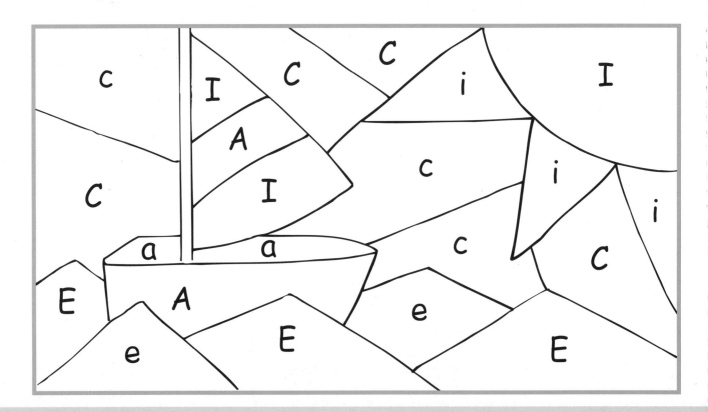

See Them Bloom!

 1 red   2 orange   3 yellow   4 green   5 blue   6 purple

Count the flowers. Write the number of flowers on the pot.
Color each set the correct color.

Puzzle Time

Look at each picture. Write the word.

WORD BOX

dig	bus	bed	cab
red	dog	desk	bee

Blast Off!

Color each shape.

red

orange

blue

yellow

Look Who's Cooking

Mark all the things that start like  cup.

How many did you find?

10

Now I Know My ABC's

Connect the letters from A to Z.

See the Pattern

Continue each pattern. Read the patterns.

Use 2 colors to make your own pattern.

12

An Elephant Snack

Use the code to crack the secret message.

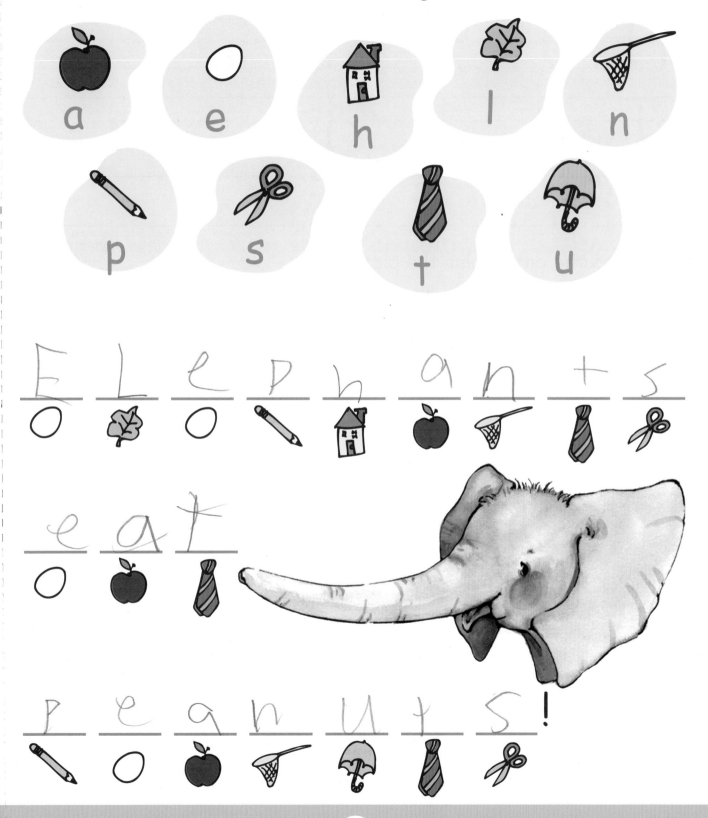

Just Hovering!

Trace each letter.

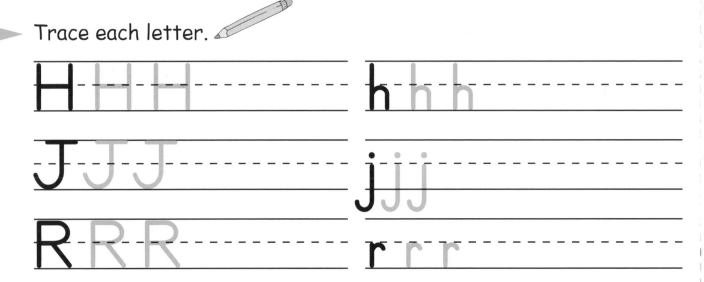

H H H   h h h

J J J   j j j

R R R   r r r

Connect the dots. Color the picture.

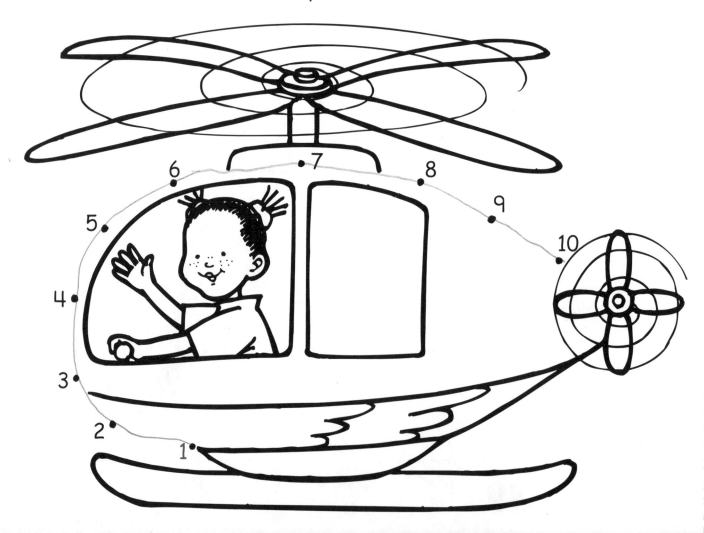

Finish It!

Draw and color the missing part.

15

Mind Your P's and Q's

Trace each letter.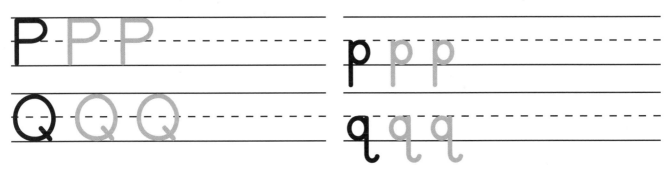

P P P

p p p

Q Q Q

q q q

Circle the letters that are the same.

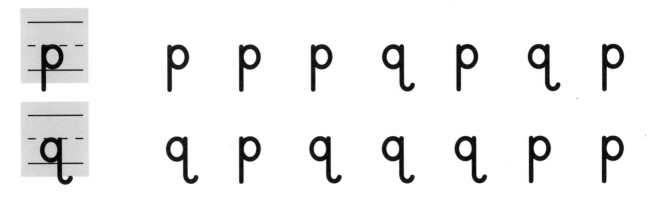

p p p p q p q p

q q p p q q q p p

Follow the p's to get through the maze.

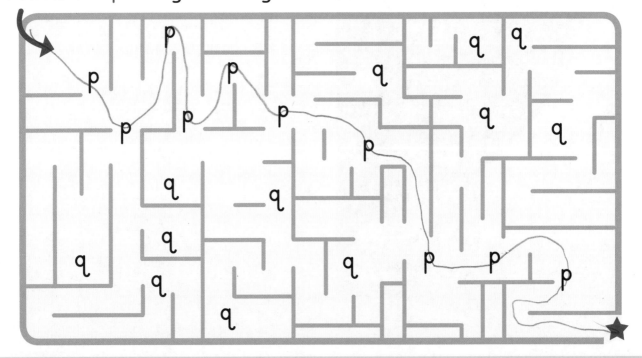

Make a Book

Cut out the pages. Put them in order. Read the book.

1 One long tail,

3 tiny feet—

5 One longer tail,

7 Watch out, little mouse.

staple
staple

4 This little mouse smells cheese to eat.

2 sharp nose,

8 It's a cat surprise!

6 two bright green eyes,

Fun in the Sand

Cut and paste to match the number word with its number.

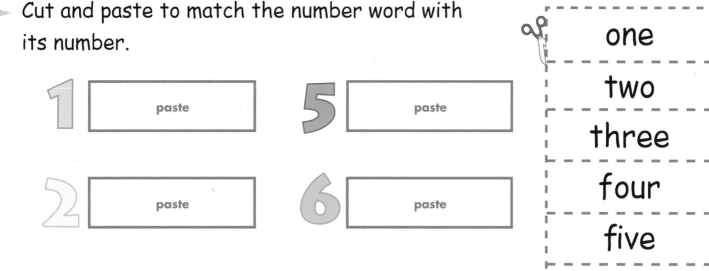

1 | paste   5 | paste

2 | paste   6 | paste

3 | paste   7 | paste

4 | paste   8 | paste

one

two

three

four

five

six

seven

eight

Read the poem. Write the answer.

One little boy jumped in the sand.
Two more came to lend a hand.
Three little girls began to play.
How many in all are here today?

Mystery Animal

▶ Write the missing letter to complete each word. Use each letter in the box 1 time.

h	i	o	p	p

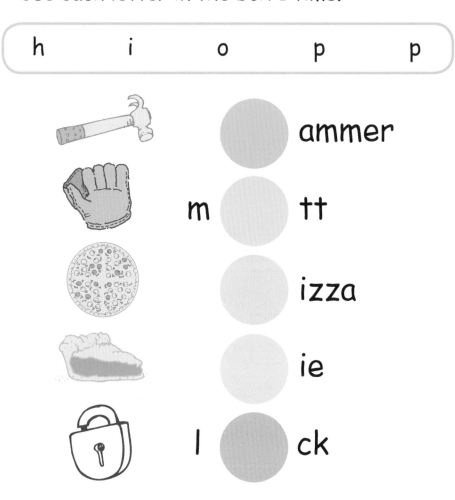

( ) ammer

m ( ) tt

( ) izza

( ) ie

l ( ) ck

▶ Read the word in the circles. Circle the animal named.

I Can Spell!

Trace each letter.

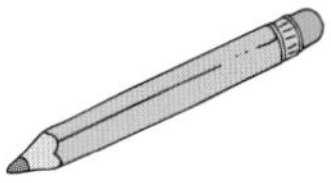

S S S

s s s

X X X

x x x

Choose s or x to finish each word.

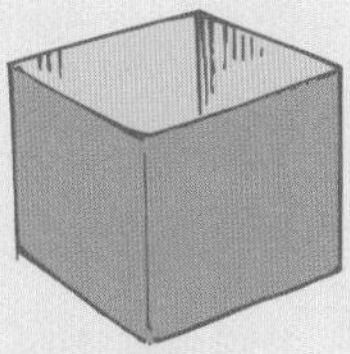

bo___

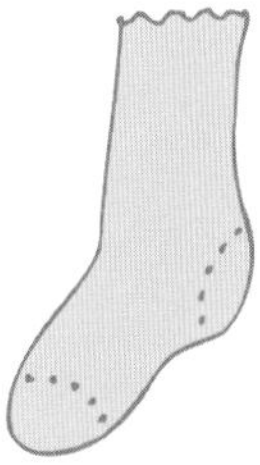

___ock

fo___

___eal

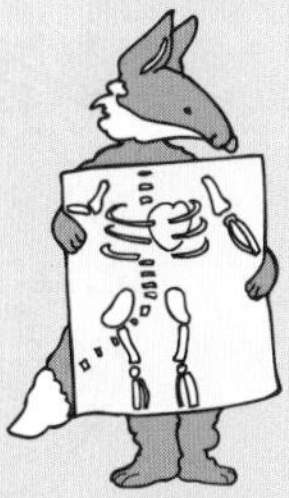

___-ray

lip___

kid___

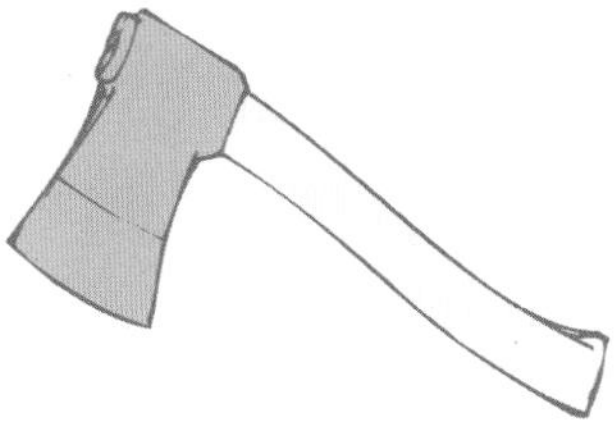

a___

___ick

What Time Is It?

Write the time shown on each clock. Fill in the boxes.

 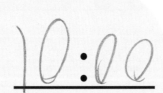 **10:00**

time to

e a d r

r	e	a	d

  **6:00**

time to

t e a

e	a	t

   **9:00**

time for

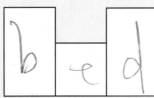

e d b

b	e	d

  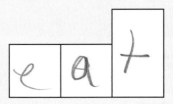 **3:00**

time for

l p y a

p	l	a	y

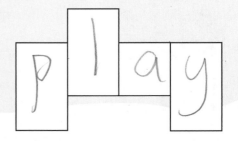

Three in a Row

Make 3 in a row by coloring the 3 letters that are the same.

e	a	t
r	e	g
n	f	e

x	b	v
m	m	m
u	z	a

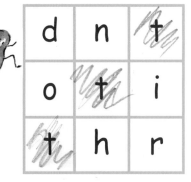

d	n	t
o	t	i
t	h	r

q	q	q
i	d	f
u	v	k

p	x	s
y	x	m
r	x	e

j	u	y
j	k	d
j	s	q

T	Y	G
Z	G	Q
G	H	L

C	V	I
B	M	K
G	G	G

K	Z	L
A	K	D
Q	S	K

E	P	Y
T	P	W
R	P	L

O	O	O
Z	E	W
S	K	L

R	C	H
T	G	H
O	Y	H

The Long and Short of It

shorter?   longer?   shorter?   longer?   shorter?   longer?

Draw something that is shorter than your arm.

Draw something that is longer than your foot.

24

Beautiful Butterfly

Trace each letter.

B B B

b b b

D D D

d d d

Color the picture.

d = yellow

b = blue

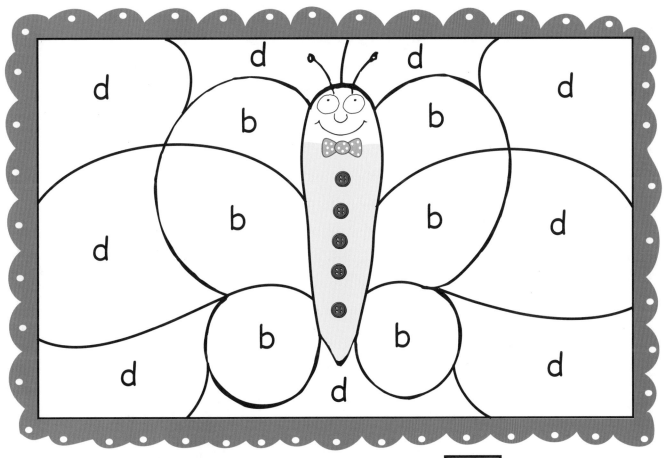

d   d

d   d

b   b

b   b

d   d

d

b   b

d   d

d

Does begin with b or d? ☐

Spin the Wheel

Use a paper clip and a pencil to make a spinner.

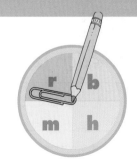

1. Spin the spinner and write the letter on one of the lines.
2. Draw a picture to show what the word means.

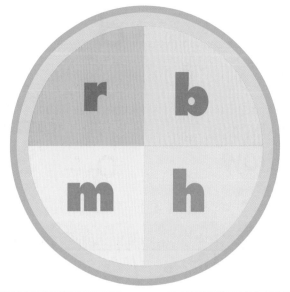

___ug	___ug
___ug	___ug

Flutter By

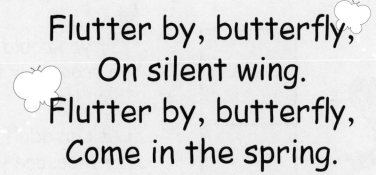

Flutter by, butterfly,
On silent wing.
Flutter by, butterfly,
Come in the spring.

What rhymes with flutter by?　　What rhymes with spring?

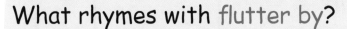

Cut out the butterfly. Tape it to a pencil. Move it up and down to make the wings flutter. Make it fly as you read the poem.

How Tall?

The average frog jumps 20 times its height.

The frog is _____ blocks tall.
It can hop 60 blocks in one leap.

If you could hop like a frog, how far could you hop?

Ask an adult to help:
- Measure your height.
- Multiply by 20.

That's how far you could hop!

What's Missing?

Write the missing letter to complete each word. Use each letter in the box 1 time.

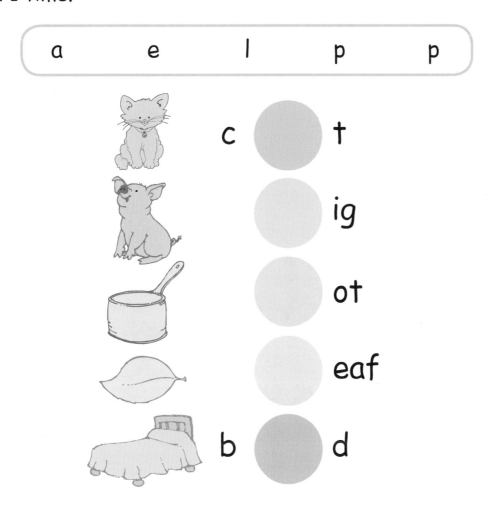

| a | e | l | p | p |

c ◯ t

◯ ig

◯ ot

◯ eaf

b ◯ d

Read the word in the circles. What is the mystery fruit?

What's Up?

Solve the problems. Then connect the dots. Start with 1.

$1 + 2 =$ ☐ •

$1 + 1 =$ ☐ •

$0 + 1 =$ ☐

$1 + 3 =$ ☐ •

$1 + 4 =$ ☐

$5 + 5 =$ ☐

$2 + 4 =$ ☐ •

$4 + 4 =$ ☐ •

$5 + 4 =$ ☐ •

$3 + 4 =$ ☐

It's a _____ .

Dinner's Ready!

Start at the stove. Color the boxes with food words. Make a path to reach the dinner table.

cap		mitten	boat	boot
butterfly	apple	giraffe	snake	monkey
cupcake	bananas	fox	bat	dog
cookies	mouse	lion	kitten	goat
egg	fries	skunk	jam	toast
owl	carrot	hot dog	ice cream	

31

The Baby

Choose the correct picture. Make the poem rhyme.

Kicking feet with tiny _____,

Waving fists and a baby _____,

Soft pink cheeks and big blue _____,

First he coos and then he _____.

At the Circus

Connect the dots to discover the circus animal. Start with A. Color the picture.

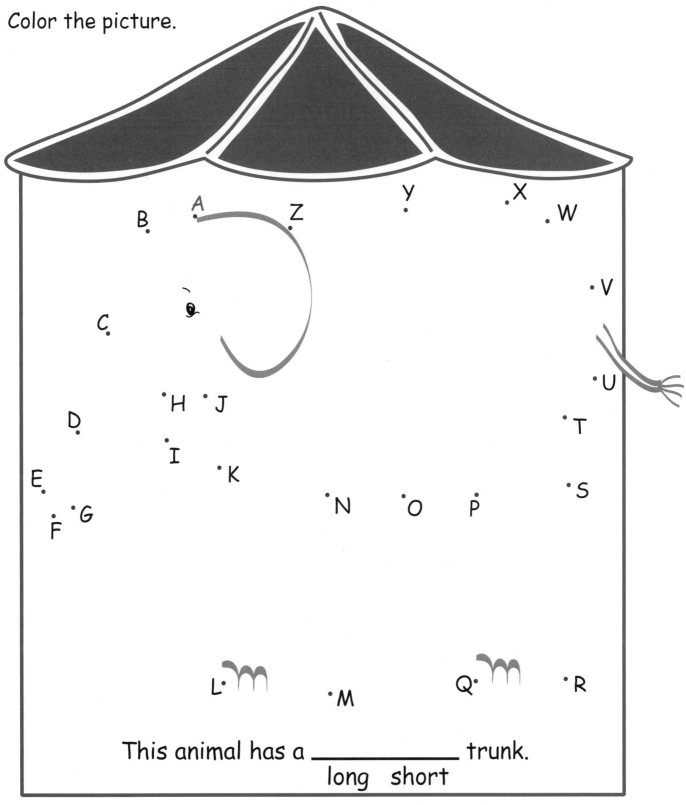

This animal has a _____ trunk.

long   short

Picking Up Pennies!

Money

Help Peter get to the Popcorn Palace. Follow the pennies. Each time he passes a penny in the path, Peter picks it up and puts it in his pouch. When he gets to the Popcorn Palace, help him decide what to buy.

What will Peter buy? Make sure that he has enough money for the thing or things you choose.

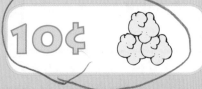  

A Rainbow of Hats

Unscramble each color word. Color the hats.

red   orange   yellow   green

blue   purple   pink   brown

eubl — blue

npik — pink

pprule — purple

dre — red

angeor — orange

lloywe — yellow

orbwn — brown

eergn — green

Change the Story

Read .
Replace each green word with its opposite in ②.
Read ②.

① The little boy went up the ladder.

He stopped at the top.

He looked down.

Then he waved hello.

② The little boy went _____ the ladder.

He stopped at the _____ .

He looked _____ .

Then he waved _____ .

WORD BOX

bottom   up   good-bye   down

Choose a good name for ①.

On Top   Climbing   The Picnic

Choose a good name for ②.

The Tree House   Climbing   The Ride

Find the Twins

Cut out the giraffes. Paste each one by its twin.

	paste
	paste
paste	paste
	paste
 paste	 paste

Circus Math

Use the elephant and the clown from page 38 to help you find the answers.

Draw the answer here.

How many legs do two elephants and one clown have in all?

10 legs

How many tails do three elephants and two clowns have in all?

tails

How many ears do three clowns and two elephants have in all?

ears

How many fingers do two elephants and three clowns have in all?

fingers

Lines and Circles

Trace each letter.

K K K   k k k

L L L   l l l

E E E   e e e

Y Y Y   y y y

Z Z Z   z z z

O O O   o o o

Write the answers to the questions.

How can you find something that is lost using only your eyes?

Where can you find a roaring lion and a snoring hippo?

What can you do at the ballgame but not at the library?

WORD BOX

zoo   yell   look

The Hungry Ant

Paste the pictures in ABC order. Then read the story.

Look at the [paste] . **A**

The ant eats the [paste] . **B**

The ant eats the [paste] . **C**

The ant eats the [paste] . **D**

The ant eats the [paste] . **E**

The ant is [paste] .  **F**

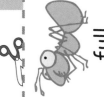 full

 cookie

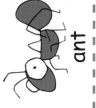 egg

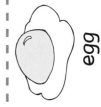 ant

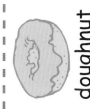 doughnut

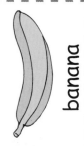 banana

Puzzle Time

Look at each picture. Write the word.

tub

slug

jug

mug

cub

sub

club

gum

WORD BOX

club	gum	jug	cub
sub	mug	slug	tub

A Snowy Day

Mark the things Carlos should wear to build a snowman.

43

Ready for Fun!

Read the sentences. Add the things to the picture.

I have one green hat.

I have two purple bags.

I have three orange flowers.

I have four purple balloons.

I have five blue pockets.

I have one red lollipop in each pocket.

I'm ready for fun!

On My Street

Solve each math problem. Color the picture.

1   2   3   4   5

4 + 1

0 + 1

1 + 1

3 + 2

2 + 0

2 + 1

0 + 3

1 + 1

$\begin{array}{r} 2 \\ + 2 \\ \hline \end{array}$

0 + 2

1 + 0

1 + 4

A Riddle

Solve each math problem. Use the code to answer the riddle. Write the letter that goes with each answer on the line.

a   0   e   1   n   2   p   3   r   4   s   5   w   6

What is black and white and read all over?

$$\begin{array}{r} 1 \\ -1 \\ \hline 0 \end{array} \quad \boxed{a}$$

$$\begin{array}{r} 2 \\ -0 \\ \hline \square \end{array}$$

$$\begin{array}{r} 4 \\ -3 \\ \hline \square \end{array}$$

$$\begin{array}{r} 6 \\ -0 \\ \hline \square \end{array}$$

$$\begin{array}{r} 6 \\ -1 \\ \hline \square \end{array}$$

$$\begin{array}{r} 4 \\ -1 \\ \hline \square \end{array}$$

$$\begin{array}{r} 3 \\ -3 \\ \hline \square \end{array}$$

$$\begin{array}{r} 5 \\ -2 \\ \hline \square \end{array}$$

$$\begin{array}{r} 2 \\ -1 \\ \hline \square \end{array}$$

$$\begin{array}{r} 4 \\ -0 \\ \hline \square \end{array}$$

Answer: _____

A Word Search

Find the words and circle them.

```
H A M B U R G E R E P S
Z E B R A P J M C T P Q
R U D O W X P S B R Z I
O H C O W E C W W T E I
C B P E A S Q V O L K H
M N D I T T R E E I P Y
W S H Y D B U N N Y B W
A L L I G A T O R R I C
N F H X O Z D G R A S S
M J M U N F L O W E R J
R N P K A S C Q W M T M
G R A P E S J U O J Y Q
```

WORD BOX

alligator	cow	flower	grapes	grass
hamburger	peas	tree	zebra	bunny

Under the Sea

Solve each problem. Use the color key to color the picture.

green = 0   orange = 1   yellow = 2   blue = 3

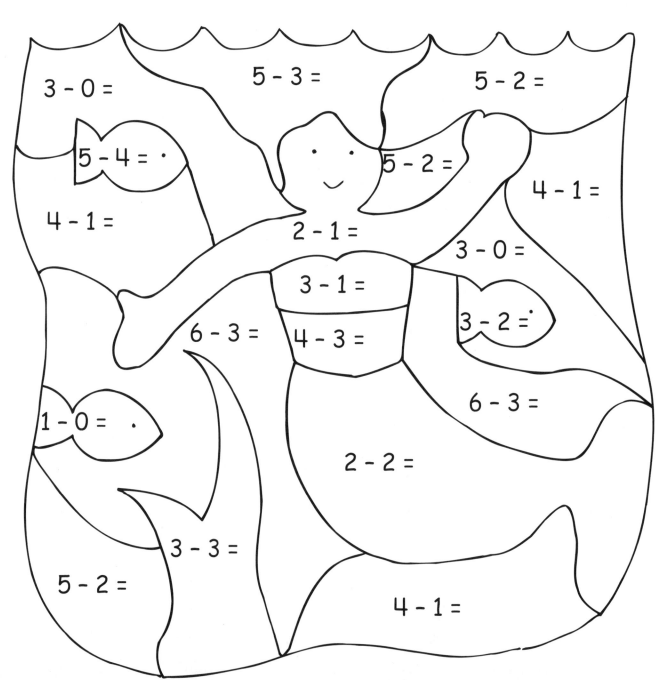

Riding a Bike

Cut the pages. Make the book. Read the story.

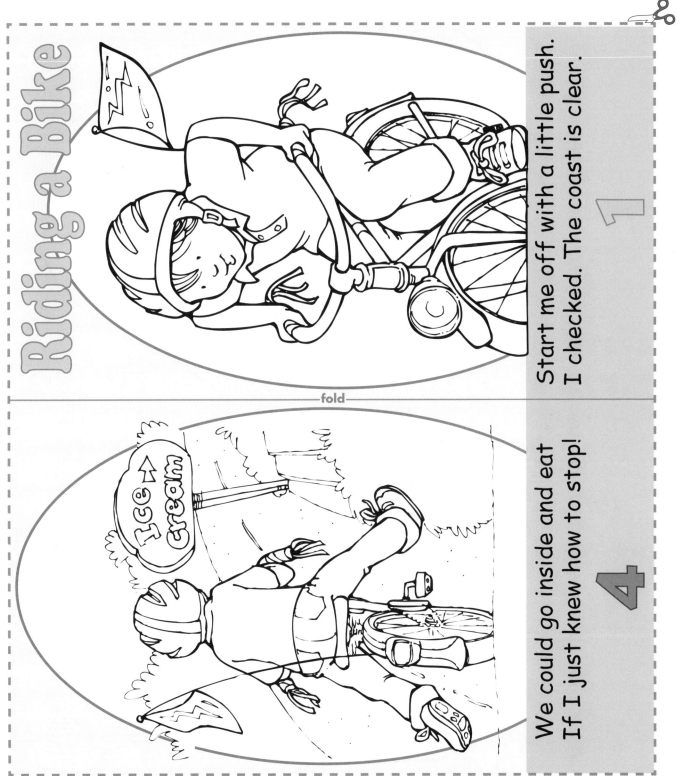

Riding a Bike

fold

Start me off with a little push.
I checked. The coast is clear.

1

We could go inside and eat
If I just knew how to stop!

4

2

I can make the pedals work,
And I've learned how to steer.

fold

3

Let's ride along the bike path
And stop at the ice-cream shop.

EMC 6309 • © Evan-Moor Corp.

Follow the Balloons

Color the balloons that have the short e sound like you hear in  .

How many balloons
did you color?

Here Kitty, Kitty

Read each sentence. Draw Kitty in each picture.

Kitty is on the bed.

Kitty is up the tree.

Kitty is under the desk.

Kitty is in the tub.

How Many Spots?

In each circle, count the number of spots on Dog 1 and write the number. Draw 1 less spot on Dog 2 and write the number.

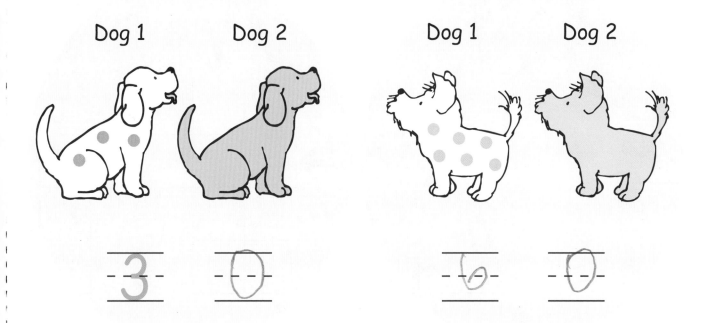

Dog 1   Dog 2   Dog 1   Dog 2

3   0   6   0

Dog 1   Dog 2   Dog 1   Dog 2

2   0   5   0

Happy Day

Count the smiles. Write the number word in the puzzle.

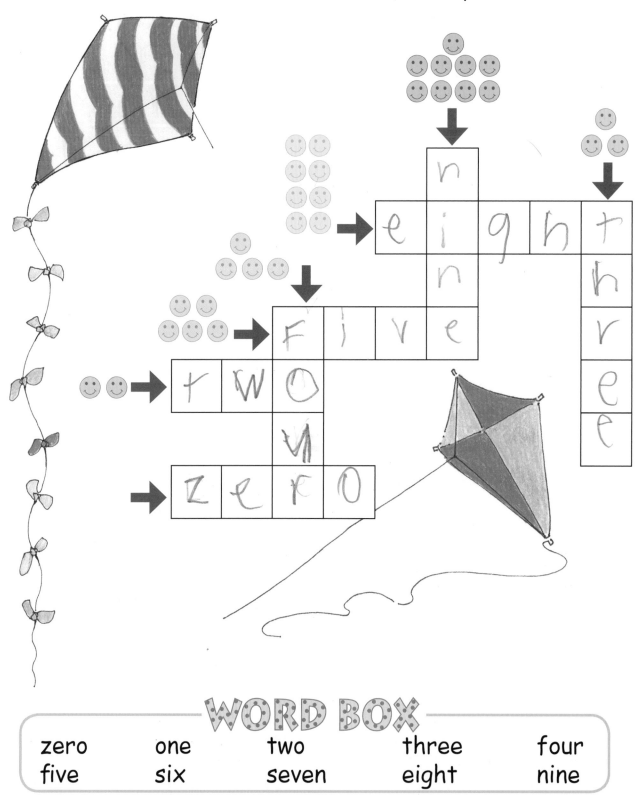

WORD BOX

zero	one	two	three	four
five	six	seven	eight	nine

Koala Puppet

Cut out this koala puppet and ears. Fold on the line.
Paste the edge closed. Paste on the ears.

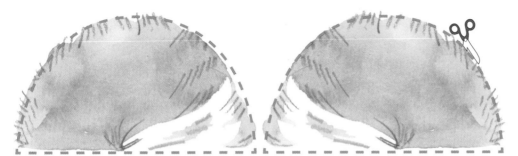

Koalas live in
special trees.
Eucalyptus!
They like to eat the
tasty leaves.

Put Koala on your hand.
Tell about her home in
Australia.

paste

paste

fold

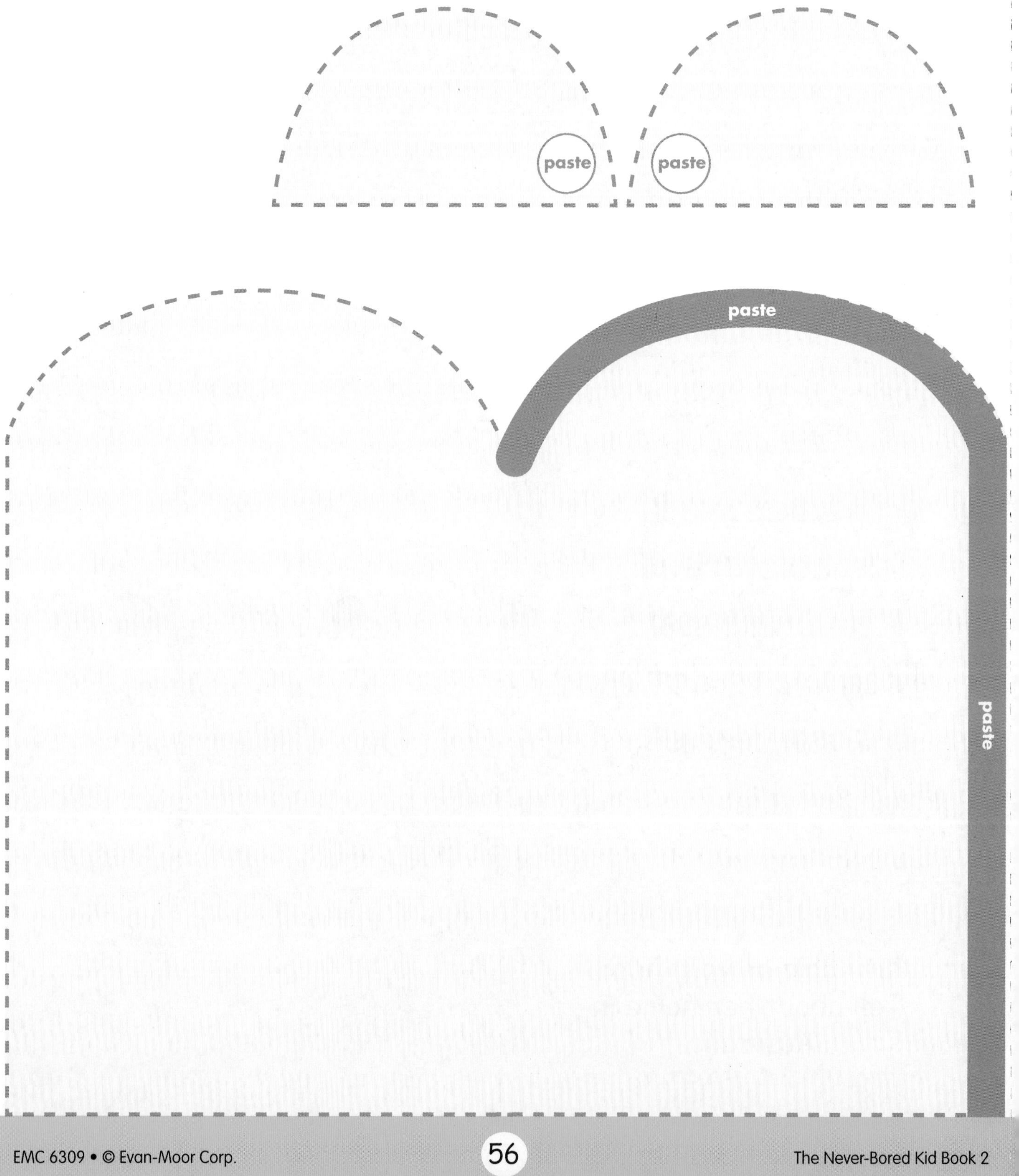

paste

paste

paste

paste

Sharing a Treat

Making a Graph, Fractions

Count the equal-sized pieces of each treat.

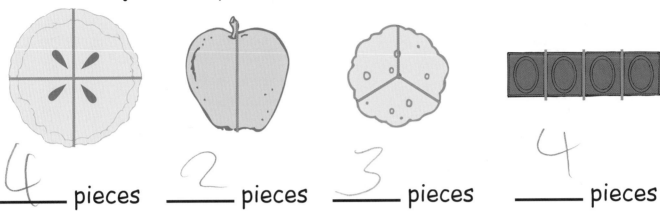

_4_ pieces   _2_ pieces   _3_ pieces   _4_ pieces

Complete the graph to show how many pieces.

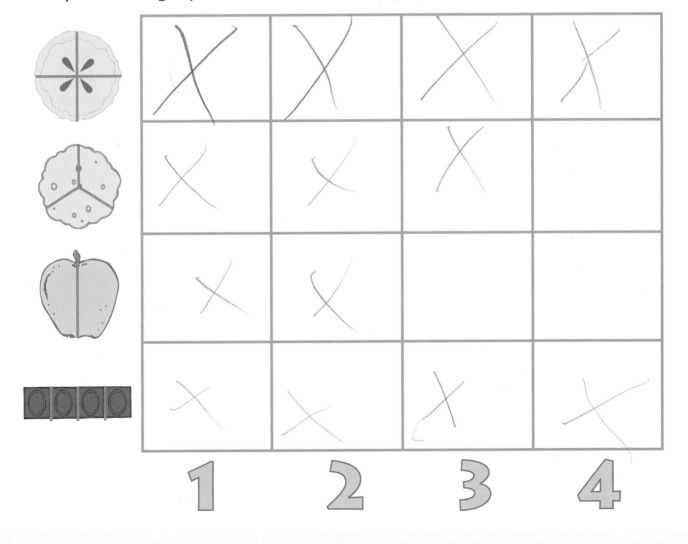

Lots of Colors

Write the name of the color in each box.

WORD BOX

black	blue	brown	gray	green	orange
pink	purple	red	white	yellow	

A Celebration

Comprehension

Cut the pages. Make a little book. Read the story.

staple

staple

1

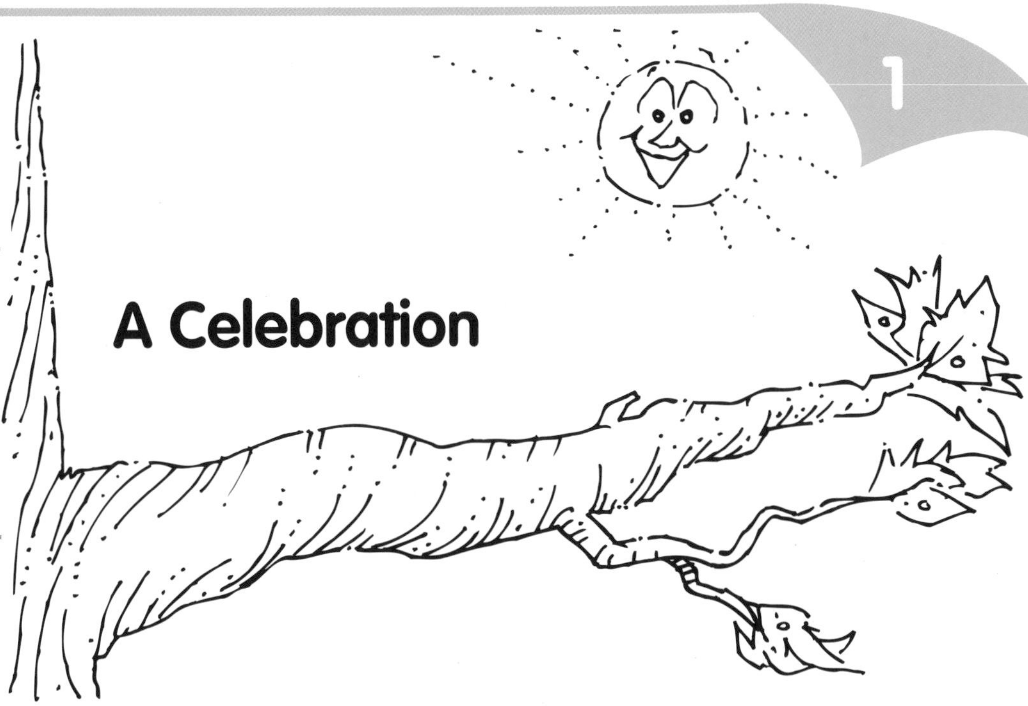

A Celebration

3

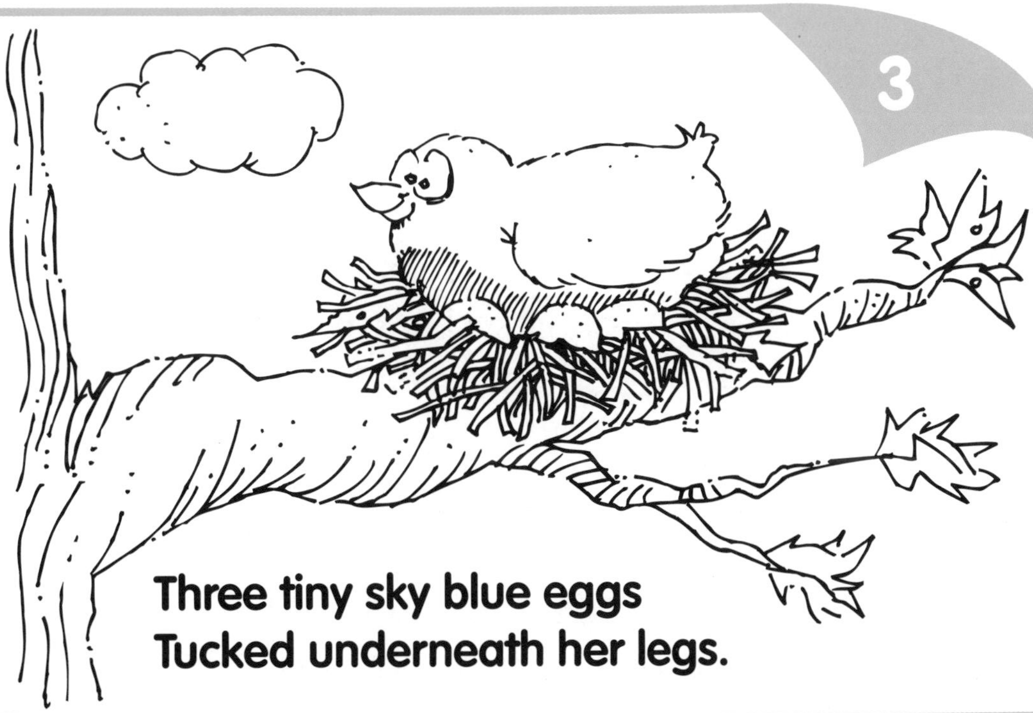

Three tiny sky blue eggs
Tucked underneath her legs.

2

Sticks and mud
and dry, brown grass
Make a robin's nest first class!

4

Mother Robin sits and waits.
Then, of course, she celebrates.

People, Places, and Things

A noun names a person, a place, or a thing. Cut out the pictures and paste these nouns under the correct heading.

PEOPLE   PLACES   THINGS

61

What Colors Do You See?

Find each word.

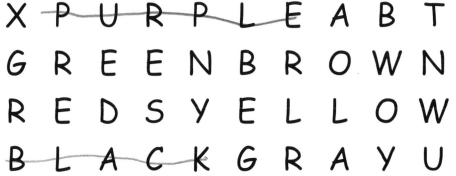

```
X  P  U  R  P  L  E  A  B  T
G  R  E  E  N  B  R  O  W  N
R  E  D  S  Y  E  L  L  O  W
B  L  A  C  K  G  R  A  Y  U
B  L  U  E  O  R  A  N  G  E
W  H  I  T  E  N  P  I  N  K
```

WORD BOX

black	blue	brown	gray	green	orange
pink	purple	red	white	yellow	

Parents and Babies

Cut and paste. Match each parent with its baby.

Riddles, Riddles, Riddles

Draw a line from the riddle to the answer.

Where do fish keep their money?

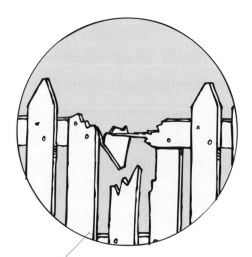

time to fix the fence

What time is it when an elephant sits on your fence?

in the riverbank

Counting Coins

Circle the coins needed to buy each item.

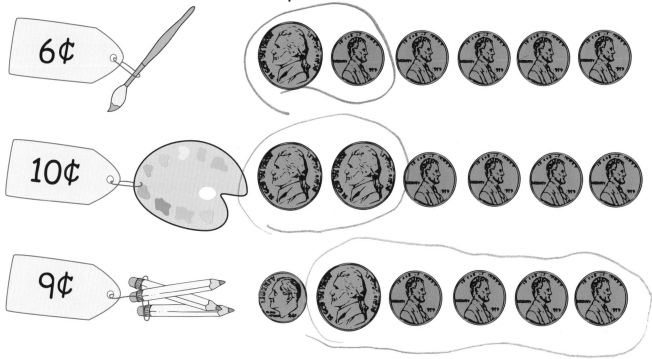

Color only the coins to find the secret message.

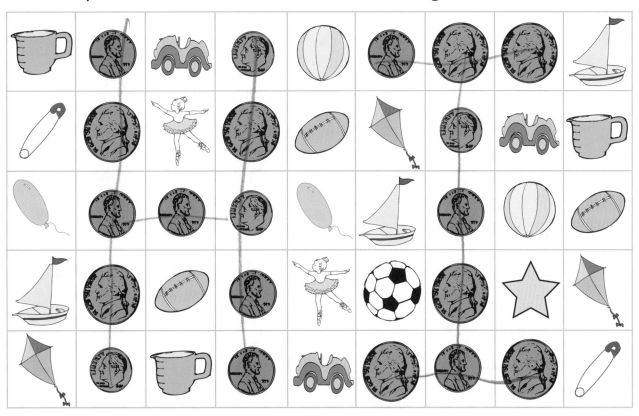

65

Wheel of Words

Spin the wheel and read the word. Color the same word on the board and spin again. You win the game when you have colored 4 words in a row.

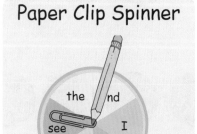

Paper Clip Spinner

Place a paper clip on the center of the spinner and hold in place with a pencil.

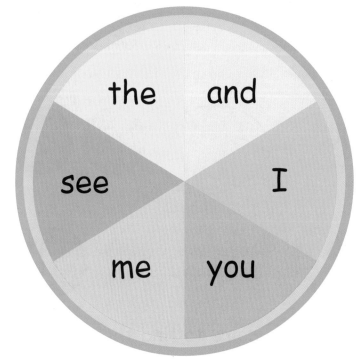

and	I	and	see
me	the	me	you
see	I	you	the
the	see	and	I

Where Are My Shoes?

Write the location of each shoe.

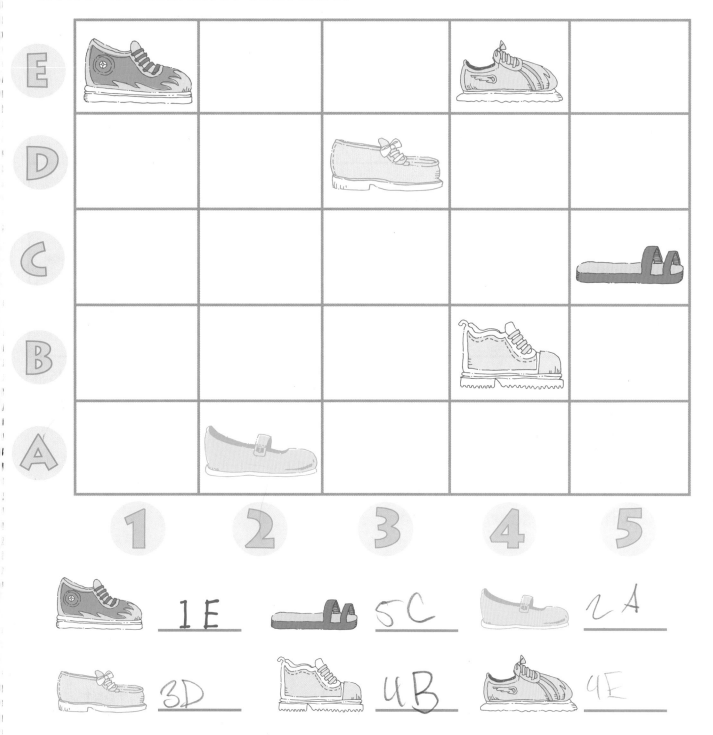

Draw another shoe in an empty square.
Where did you put it? _____

Dandy Dinosaurs

Use the information on the chart to answer the questions.

50
40
30
20
10

Brachiosaurus   Triceratops   Stegosaurus   Tyrannosaurus Rex

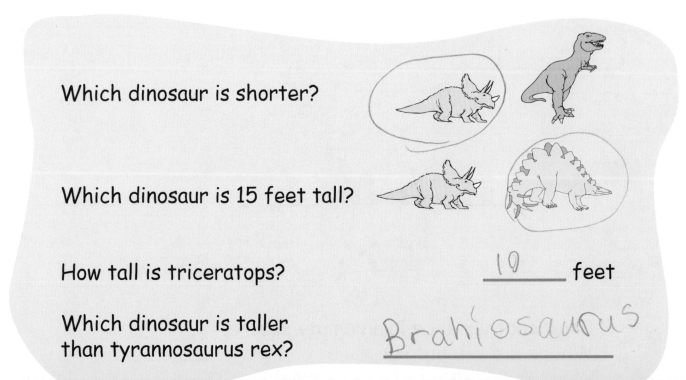

Which dinosaur is shorter?

Which dinosaur is 15 feet tall?

How tall is triceratops? _____10_____ feet

Which dinosaur is taller
than tyrannosaurus rex?   Brahiosaurus

Friends Come in Many Sizes

Reading Words

Cut the pages. Make the book. Read the story. ✂

Friends Come in Many Sizes

staple

staple

1

Friends can be tall or short. Their size doesn't matter.

3

Friends can be old or young. Their age doesn't matter.

5

Fast or slow, tall or short, loud or quiet, old or young, near or far away—the important thing about friends is that they care about you and you care about them.

7

Friends can be loud or quiet.
Their volume doesn't matter.

Friends can be fast or slow.
Their speed doesn't matter.

Draw a picture of some of your friends.

Friends can be near or far away.
Where they are doesn't matter.

Soft? White?

Cut and paste. Put the things in the section of the diagram where they belong.

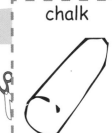
chalk

only white

paste | paste

soft and white

paste | paste

paste | paste

only soft

mitten

marshmallow

bunny

puppy

paper

Piggy Banks

▶ Draw a line matching each coin to its name.

dime   penny   quarter   nickel

▶ How much money is in each piggy bank?

_____¢   _____¢

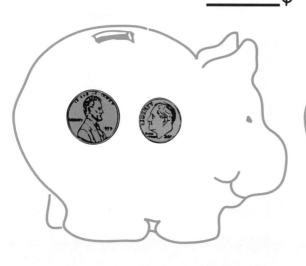   

_____¢   _____¢

A Scrambled Sentence

Cut and paste the words to make a sentence.
Color the picture.

paste	paste	paste	paste
paste	paste	paste	paste

in

cozy

bird

slept

bed.

little

The

his

Big Bears and Little Bears

Draw a big bear. Draw several little bears.

Taking Care of Your Body

Reading Comprehension

Cut the pages. Make the book. Read the story.

staple

staple

Taking Care of Your Body

1

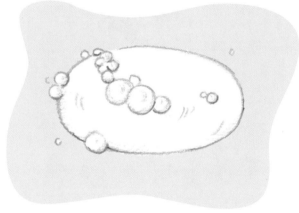

Keep your body clean.

▷ Washing with soap and water helps get rid of germs and dirt.

▷ Brushing your teeth keeps them strong and healthy.

▷ Clean hair feels good.

3

Eat healthy food.

▷ Eat five servings of fruits and vegetables every day.

▷ Too much sugar and fat can hurt your body.

▷ Milk helps bones grow.

5

► When you run or work or sing or read, the different parts of your body are working together.

► It is your job to take good care of this special machine.

2

Your body is like a machine.

► Jumping keeps your heart strong.

► It's fun to run and play.

► Fresh air is good for you.

4

Exercise every day.

► Your body needs time to rest.

► You can work better when you are rested.

► You can run faster if you get enough sleep.

6

Get plenty of sleep.

Naming Patterns

Finish labeling each pattern.

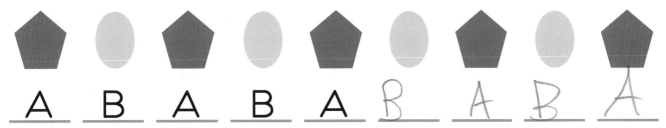

A   B   A   B   A   B   A   B   A

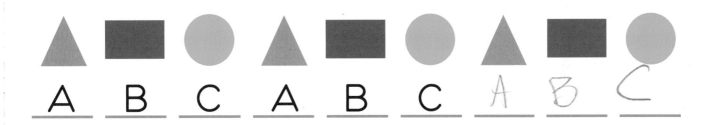

A   B   C   A   B   C   A   B   C

A   A   B   A   A   B   A   A   B

Color the stars to make a pattern. Label the pattern.

L   N   L   N   L   N

Saying the Same Thing

Synonyms are different words with the same meaning. Look at each picture. Circle the two words with the same meaning that go with the picture.

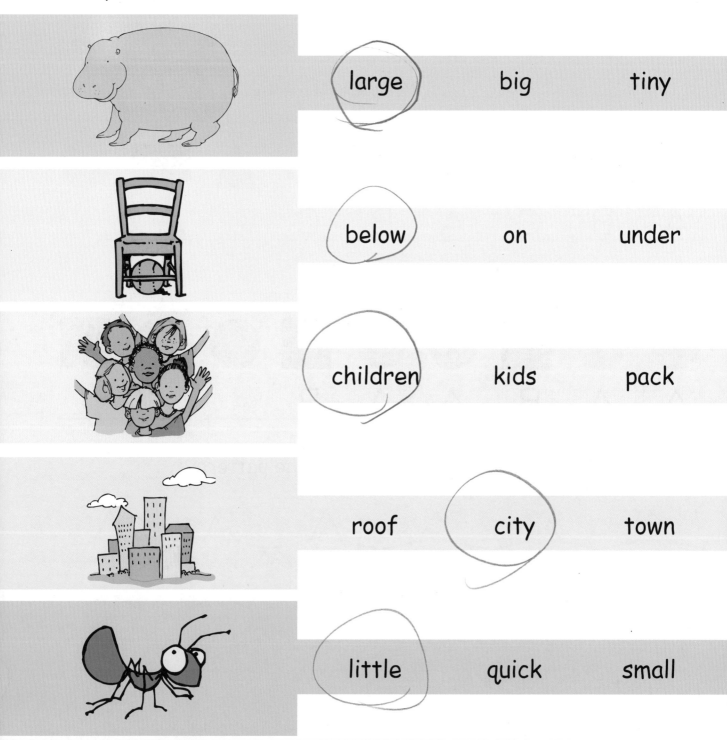

large   big   tiny

below   on   under

children   kids   pack

roof   city   town

little   quick   small

A Secret Message

Write the missing letter for each word. Then write the letter on the line with the same number.

1. <u>f</u>an

2. p<u>i</u>n

3. <u>s</u>and

4. <u>h</u>ug

5. <u>c</u>andy

6. <u>a</u>pple

7. gree<u>n</u>

8. <u>s</u>un

9. <u>w</u>agon

10. h<u>i</u>ppo

11. le<u>m</u>on

Read the secret message.

<u>f</u> <u>i</u> <u>s</u> <u>h</u>   <u>c</u> <u>a</u> <u>n</u>
1   2   3   4   5   6   7

<u>s</u> <u>w</u> <u>i</u> <u>m</u>
8   9   10   11

First or Last?

Trace the letters.

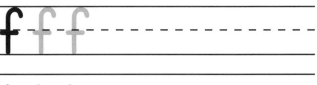

Name the pictures. Color the squares.

t at the end—red   f at the end—yellow
t at the beginning—green   f at the beginning—purple

Did you make three in a row?   yes   no

Two Scoops

Contractions

Cut out the scoops of ice cream. Glue the 2 scoops to show the words that make the contraction on each ice-cream cone.

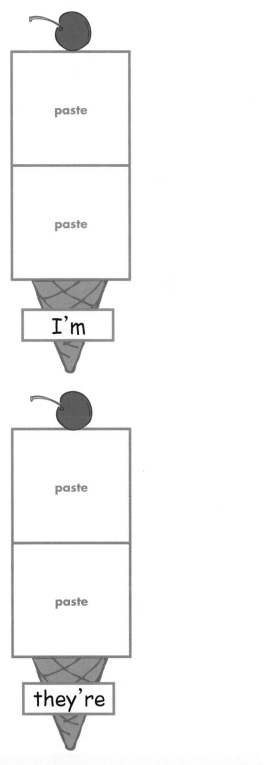

Mr. Smiles

Connect the dots. Start with A. Color the picture.

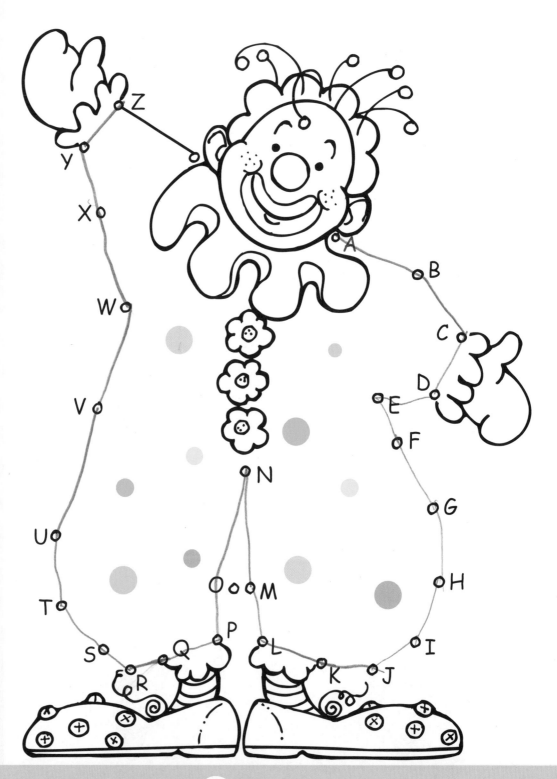

82

We Salute You

Add. Color each box.

7 = black   8 = red   9 = white   10 = blue

7 + 0	5 + 5	4 + 6	7 + 3	8 + 0	4 + 4	2 + 6
5 + 2	2 + 8	1 + 9	10 + 0	5 + 4	9 + 0	6 + 3
4 + 3	3 + 7	6 + 4	8 + 2	5 + 3	7 + 1	1 + 7
1 + 6	3 + 6	4 + 5	1 + 8	7 + 2	0 + 9	8 + 1
0 + 7	6 + 2	3 + 5	0 + 8	1 + 7	4 + 4	5 + 3
6 + 1						
2 + 5						

Places to Go

Complete the crossword puzzle.

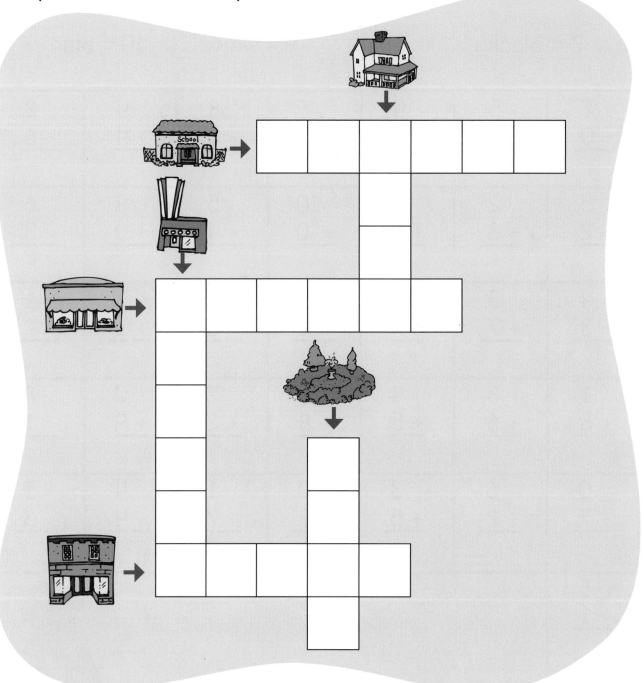

WORD BOX

home	market	park
store	movies	school

A Riddle

Read the riddle. Write the beginning letter of each picture to decode the answer.

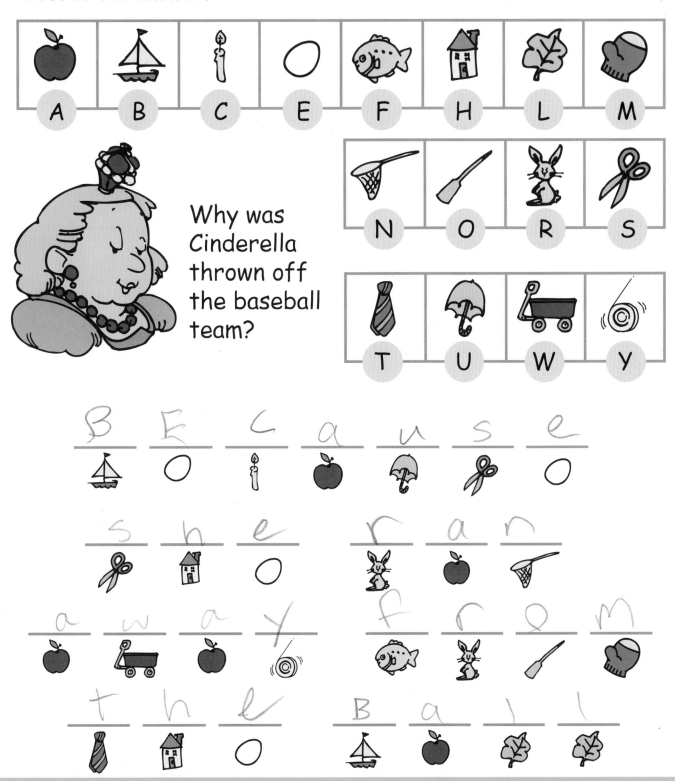

Why was Cinderella thrown off the baseball team?

B E C a u s e

s h e r a n

a w a y f r o m

t h e B a l l

Who Lives Here?

Subtract. Color the picture.

5
blue

6
brown

7
orange

10 − 5	8 − 3	9 − 4	7 − 2
	6 − 1	8 − 3	6 − 1
8 − 3	5 − 0	5 − 0	7 − 2	10 − 5
	7 − 2	10 − 4	9 − 4	5 − 0
6 − 1	9 − 4	9 − 3	10 − 5	9 − 4
	8 − 3	6 − 0	7 − 1	7 − 2
10 − 5	8 − 2	6 − 0	6 − 1
	10 − 4	10 − 3	9 − 3	

Surprise!

Read the story. Complete each sentence using the correct punctuation mark.

We went to the park ☐

It is Jon's birthday ☐

Happy Birthday, Jon ☐

Do you see a surprise ☐

It is a surprise for Jon ☐

If you do, yell SURPRISE ☐

period .

exclamation point !

question mark ?

Color the picture to see what the surprise is.

. = red

! = blue

? = yellow

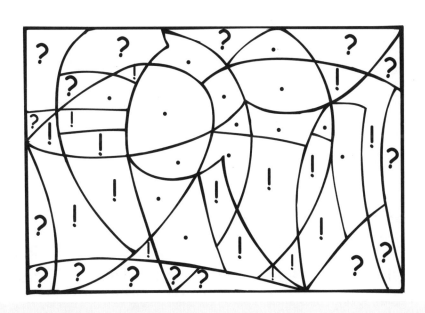

In the Ocean

Find the words in the word search.

```
S  H  A  R  K  R  S  E  X
P  E  T  B  A  P  A  M  C
R  K  E  L  P  X  N  S  D
O  T  C  O  M  E  D  W  I
C  U  B  W  A  S  Q  V  V
M  R  D  F  W  H  A  L  E
W  T  H  I  D  B  S  N  R
A  L  L  S  N  A  I  L  O
N  E  H  H  O  Z  C  G  X
M  S  E  A  W  E  E  D  W
R  N  P  K  A  S  C  Q  W
G  Z  A  P  C  L  A  M  O
```

Circle the compound words.

WORD BOX

diver	sand	whale	snail	kelp
shark	seaweed	blowfish	clam	turtles

Gone Camping

Cut out the centimeter ruler and measure each piece of camping equipment.

The lantern is

_____ cm tall.

The fishing pole is _____ cm long.

The sign is

_____ cm tall.

The tent is _____ cm long.

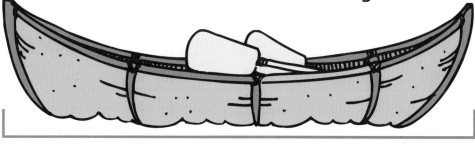

The canoe is _____ cm long.

| 1 | 2 | 3 | 4 | 5 | 6 | 7 | 8 | 9 | 10 | 11 | 12 | 13 | 14 | 15 | 16 |

7 Days

Decode each day of the week. Number the days to put them in order. Start with Sunday.

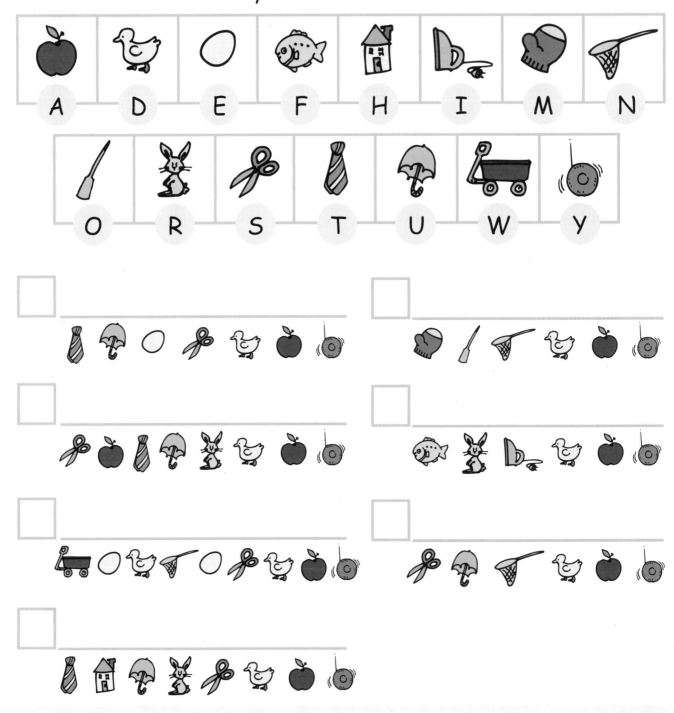

90

A Full Year

Find each month's name in the word search.

```
J A N U A R Y S N D Y D
X J U L Y S H L B Z R D
N O V E M B E R W V P E
E V F E B R U A R Y M E
N T A P R I L K H O R T
S O C T O B E R M D J V
A N R L D E C E M B E R
M A R C H C Y X O I M J
W I L H Z H J U N E T O
F A U G U S T T V K N X
A Z O B N F V Q R M A Y
S E P T E M B E R F V D
```

WORD BOX

January	February	March	April	May	June
July	August	September	October	November	December

The Mystery Shape

Make an X on any shape that fits the clues. The mystery shape will be left.

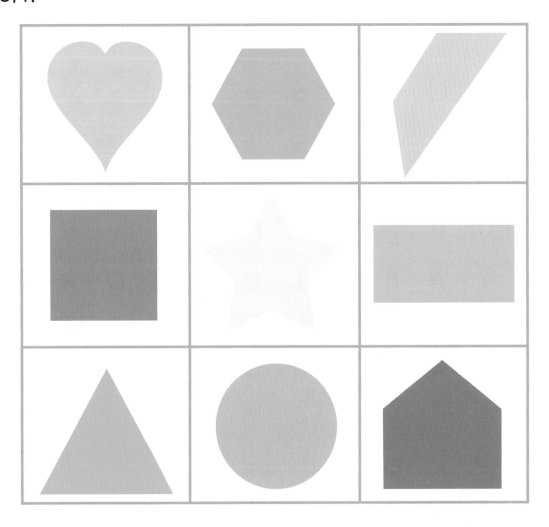

CLUES

1. I do not have any straight sides.
2. I am yellow.
3. I do not have 4 corners.
4. I have 4 sides that are not all the same size.

What shape am I? _____

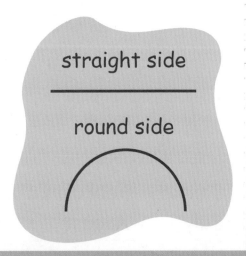

straight side
_____
round side

Begins with G

Trace each letter.

G G G

g g g

Cut and paste. Put the puzzle together.
How many things in the picture begin with a g? ☐

paste

paste

Interesting Insects

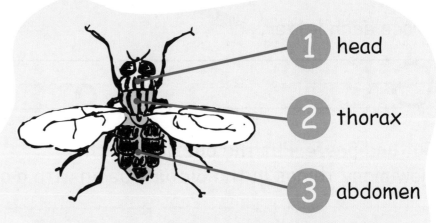

1 head
2 thorax
3 abdomen

Insects have 3 body parts and 6 legs.

Color the insects red.

Contraction Caterpillars

Cut and paste. Fill each caterpillar with the two words that make its contractions.

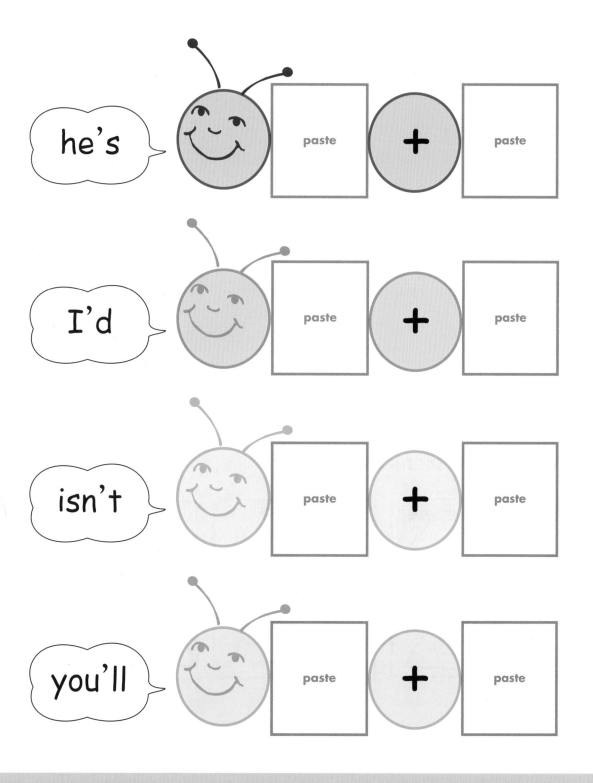

I Love Pancakes

▶ Sing this pancake song. (Sung to the tune of "Brother John")

I love pancakes.
I love pancakes.
Yes I do.
Yes I do.

I can eat them every day.
I can eat them any way.
Yes I can.
Yes I can.

▶ Number the pictures in order.

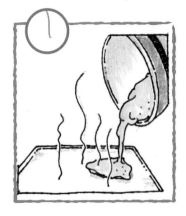

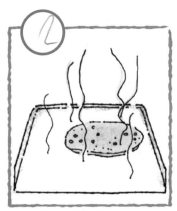

Do you like pancakes?

Riddle Me a Shape

Draw the shape that answers each riddle.

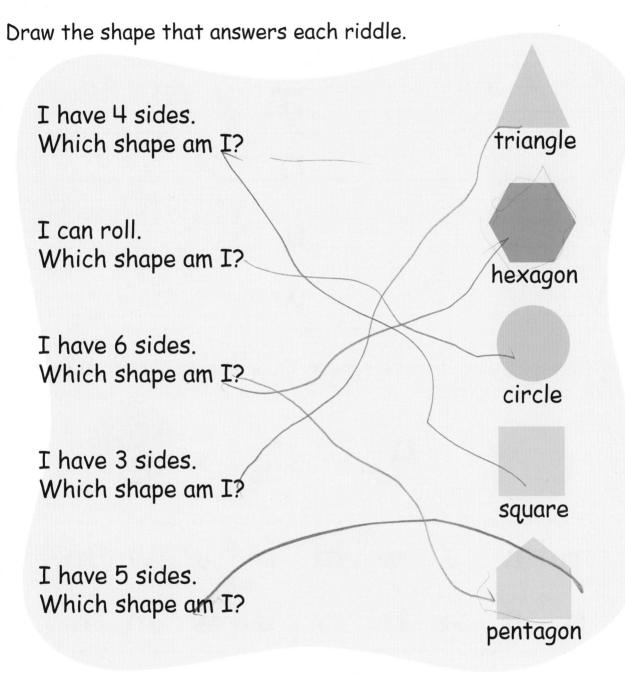

I have 4 sides.
Which shape am I?

I can roll.
Which shape am I?

I have 6 sides.
Which shape am I?

I have 3 sides.
Which shape am I?

I have 5 sides.
Which shape am I?

triangle

hexagon

circle

square

pentagon

Use 3 shapes to make a picture.

Be a Letter Detective

Trace each letter.

M M M   m m m

N N N   n n n

U U U   u u u

W W W   w w w

Some lowercase letters are similar. Color the squares to show you can read these letters:

m   n   u   w

m	n	u	w	m	n	u	w	m
n	u	w	m	n	u	w	m	n
u	w	m	n	u	w	m	n	u
w	m	n	u	w	m	n	u	w
m	n	u	w	m	n	u	w	m

Which One Is First?

Alphabetical Order

Cut out the pictures. Glue them in alphabetical order.

A B C D E F G H I J K L M
N O P Q R S T U V W X Y Z

1 | paste
2 | paste
3 | paste
4 | paste
5 | paste
6 | paste
7 | paste
8 | paste

ant

bumblebee

grasshopper

ladybug

mosquito
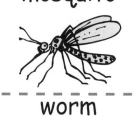

worm

spider
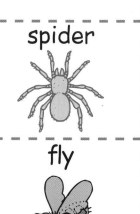

fly

All Jumbled

▶ Unscramble each word and write it on the line.

am   at   help   not   said   to   we   were

iasd _____   ma _____

ew _____   ta _____

pleh _____   wree _____

nto _____   ot _____

▶ Find and color each word in the word search.

am   at   help   not   said   to   we   were

h	e	l	p	d	u	t	o
j	p	f	a	m	e	d	c
w	e	n	o	l	n	o	t
m	g	s	a	i	d	q	k
a	t	h	i	w	e	r	e

Get in Line

Where is each animal located?

1 2 3 4 5 6

Which animal is **first** in line?

Which animal is **sixth** in line?

 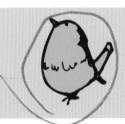

Which animal is **third** in line?

Which animal is **between the fourth and sixth** animal?

Which animal is **before the third** animal?

A Feast of Food

Use the words in the Food Bank to make compound words. Write the words. Then draw a picture of each food that you make.

FOOD BANK

cake   cheese   cup   pan   burger   cake

c u p + c a k e

cupcake

p a n + c a k e

Pancake

cheese + burger

cheeseburger

Words That Name Body Parts

Color the body part words brown.
Color the animal names blue.

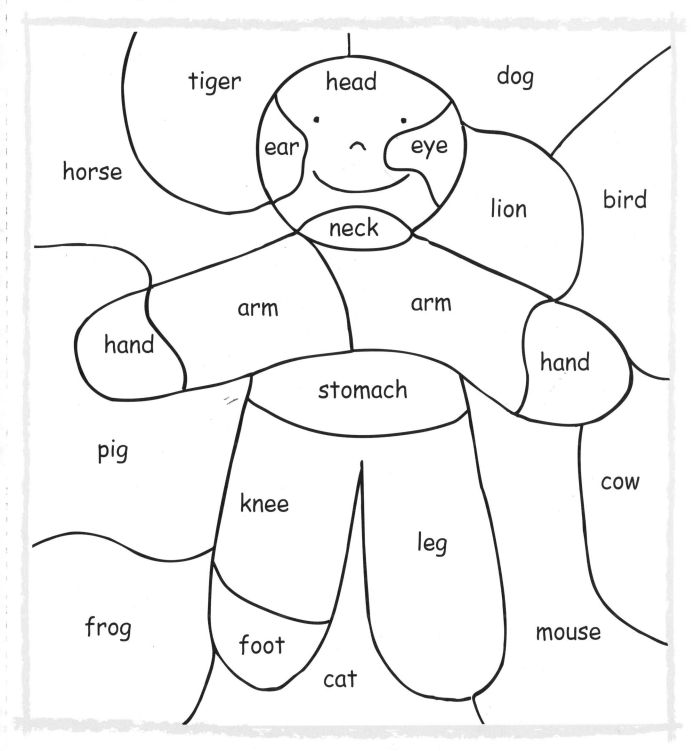

103

Hickory, Dickory, Dock

Time to the Half Hour

Connect the dots.

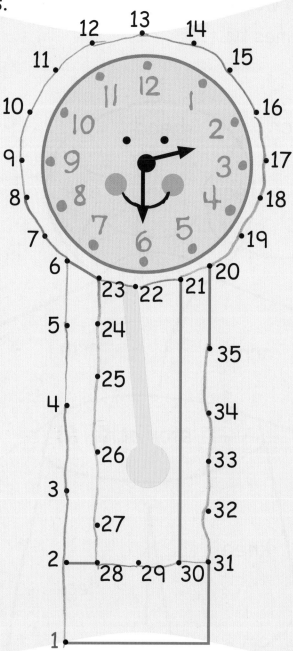

Hickory, dickory, dock.

What time is on the clock? _____

A Sleepover

Cut the pages. Make the book. ✂

staple

1

3

I'm packing up my suitcase.
Tori invited me next door.
We're going to have fun.
I'll put in a few things more.

5

I'm packing up my suitcase.
I'm going by myself, you see.
My family will stay home.
Tori called and asked just me.

7

I'm packing up my suitcase.
I just can't wait to go.
A sleepover is the very most
Exciting thing I know!

4

I'm packing up my suitcase
For a sleepover—my very first!
I'm getting so excited,
I think that I might burst!

2

I'm packing up my suitcase.
I'll put in all my stuff.
I'm taking an important trip.
I hope I brought enough.

8

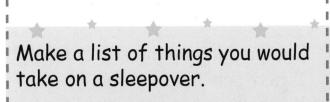

Make a list of things you would
take on a sleepover.

6

I'm packing up my suitcase.
I made a list of things to bring.
You never know when you might
Just forget to pack something.

Find the Question

Color the boxes with d red. Color the boxes with b blue.
Color the boxes with p green. Color the boxes with q yellow.

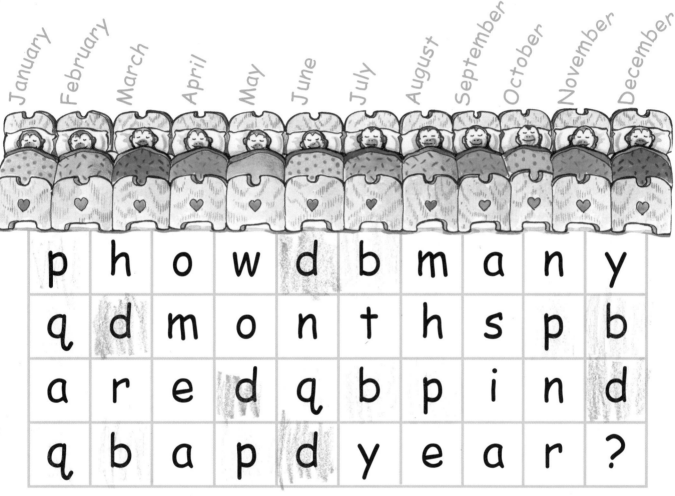

p	h	o	w	d	b	m	a	n	y
q	d	m	o	n	t	h	s	p	b
a	r	e	d	q	b	p	i	n	d
q	b	a	p	d	y	e	a	r	?

Read the white boxes. Answer the question.

how many months
are in a year?

Sam Can

Match the sentence to the picture.

Sam can run on the grass.
See Sam run.

Sam can jump over the rope.
See Sam jump.

Sam can ride on the horse.
See Sam ride.

Sam can skip on the sidewalk.
See Sam skip.

Write a sentence to tell what you can do.

On Your Mark, Get Set, Go!

Find your way to the finish line by coloring the numbers used when counting by 2s.

Start

1	0	2	4	3	5
17	10	9	6	8	7
16	2	12	11	10	12
4	15	13	18	16	14
5	6	14	20	7	8

Finish

Count by 2 to 20.

0, ___, ___, ___, ___, ___, ___, ___, ___, ___, 20

Stop-Go, Yes-No

Label each picture. Draw lines to connect the opposites.

WORD BOX

black	dry	go	in
out	stop	wet	white

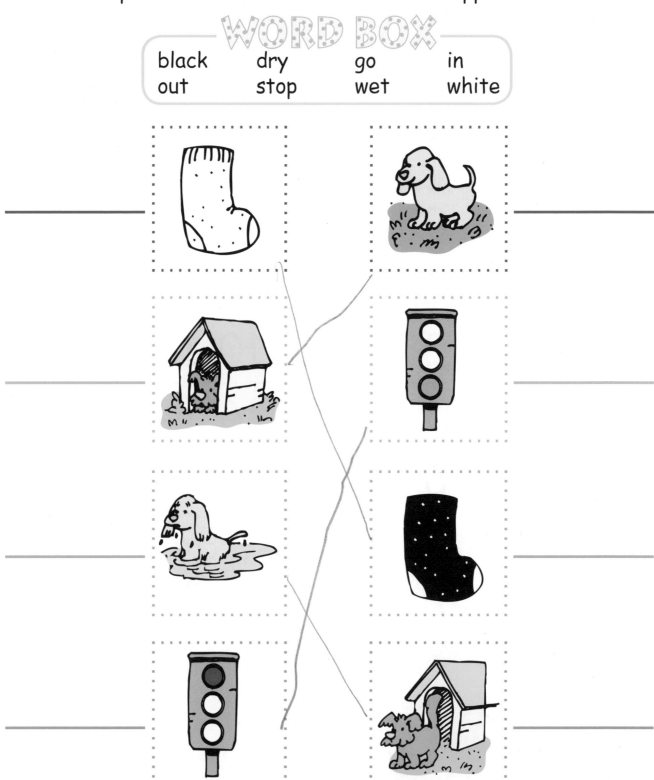

Counting by Fives

Complete the pattern by counting by 5s.

5, ___, 15, ___, 25, ___, 35, ___, 45, ___

Complete the dot-to-dot by counting by 5s. Color the picture.

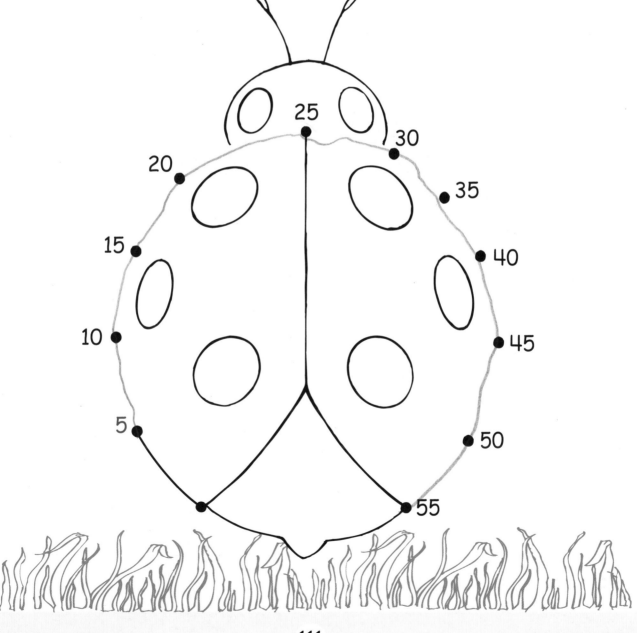

111

Hop Along, Froggy

Rhyming Words

Circle the lily pads that have two words that rhyme.

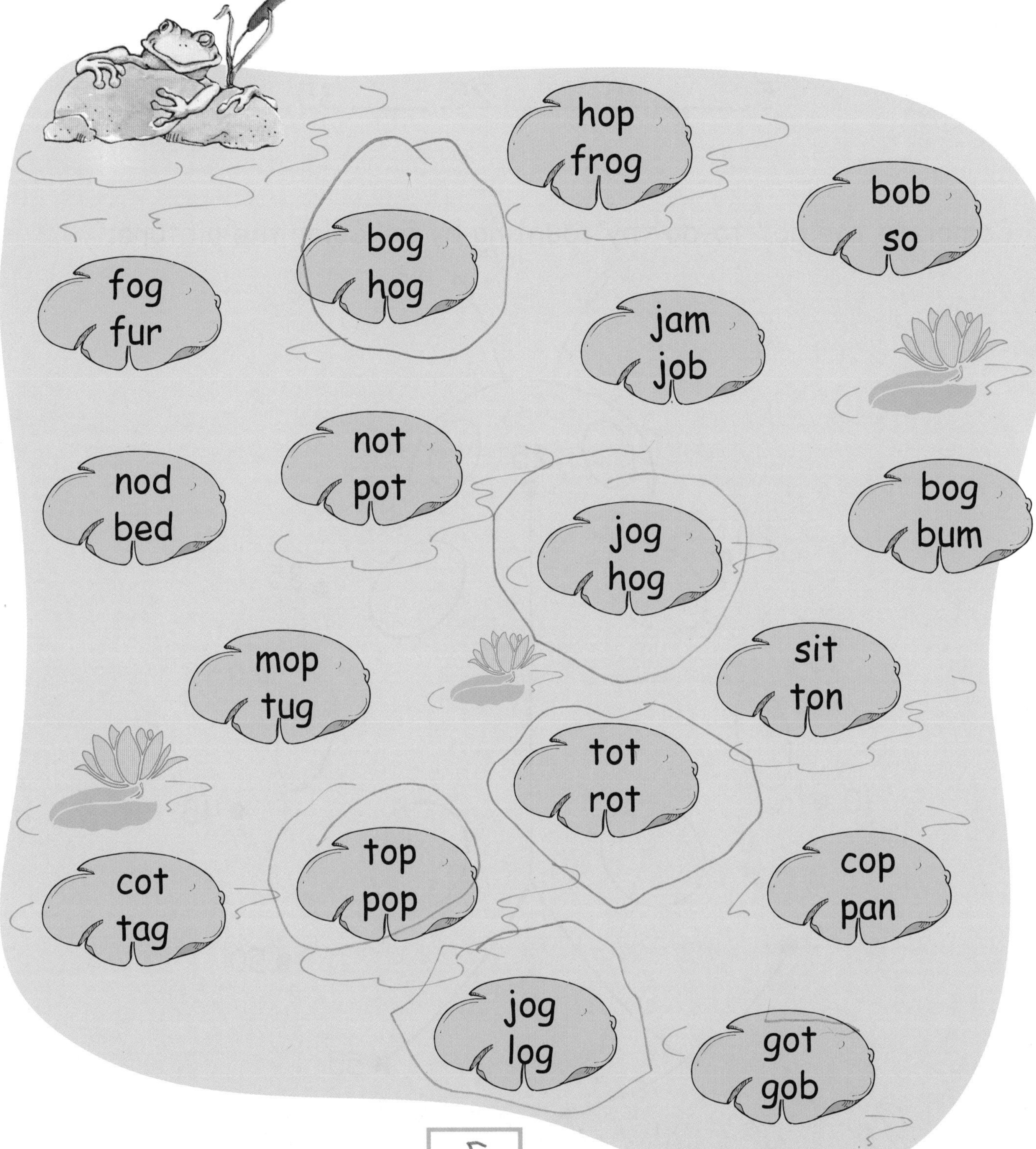
hop frog
bob so
bog hog
fog fur
jam job
not pot
nod bed
bog bum
jog hog
mop tug
sit ton
tot rot
top pop
cot tag
cop pan
jog log
got gob

How many did you circle? 5

Tic Tac Toe

Draw a line matching each picture with its name.

pot   sock   frog   mop   log   top

Look at each game. Color the three words in a line that have the short o sound.

not	hug	saw
bad	top	me
no	let	bob

be	hop	bud
see	dog	on
bug	tot	met

Write another word with a short o sound. _____

A Hundreds Chart

Write the missing numbers. Color all the squares with a 3 red. Color all the squares with a 2 blue. Color all the squares with a 4 yellow.

1	2	3	4	5	6	7	8	9	10
11	12	13	14	15	16	17	18	19	20
21	22	23	24	25	26	27	28	29	30
31	32	33	34	35	36	37	38	39	40
41	42	43	44	45	46	47	48	49	50
51	52	53	54	55	56	57	58	59	60
61	62	63	64	65	66	67	68	69	70
71	72	73	74	75	76	77	78	79	80
81	82	83	84	85	86	87	88	89	90
91	92	93	94	95	96	97	98	99	100

Which squares did you color twice?

_____

Did they change color?

yes   no

Color the rest of the squares. Make your own pattern.

Fun with Pennies

Cut and paste. Give each person 5¢.

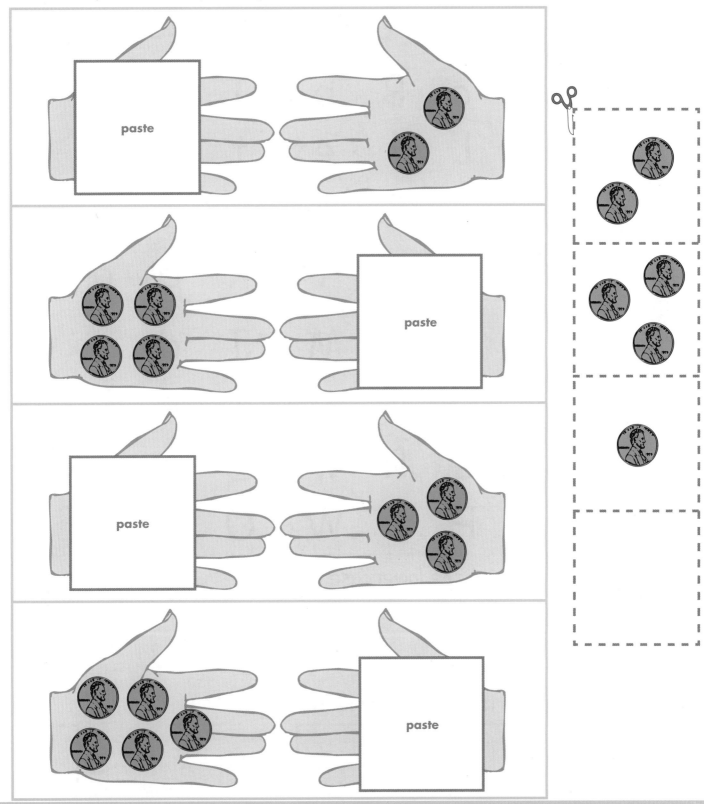

115

Big and Little

▶ Circle each pair of capital and lowercase letters.

ABCDEFGHIJKLMNOPQRSTUVWXYZ

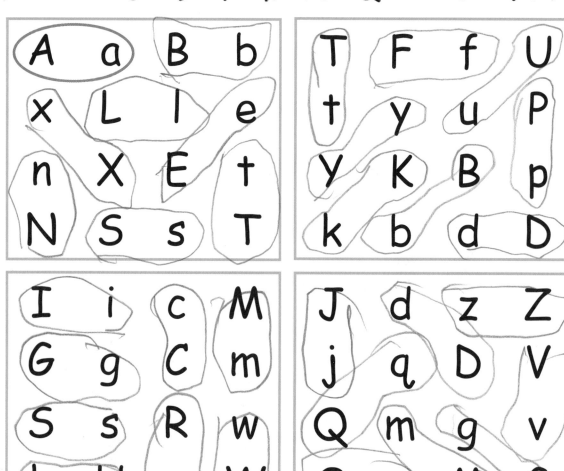

▶ Write the lowercase letter.

A    C [ ]   T [ ]   M

▶ Write the capital letter.

g [ ]   b [ ]   u [ ]   s [ ]

Words with Long e

Draw a line through the long e words in each puzzle.

long e **sound as in** feet

reach	great	like
read	hay	cub
keys	goat	race

play	beast	look
mad	eat	hop
bow	sweet	toy

beat	see	clean
tie	play	tape
new	ham	pay

cold	vase	three
not	week	cap
keep	hot	now

117

Change It!

Reading

Choose one from each box. Write a sentence. Draw a picture to show what your sentence means.

Baby Dad Mom Grandpa	ate chopped washed painted	a cookie. some weeds. the dirty dishes. the gate.

1. ______________________

____

____

2. ______________________

____

____

3. ______________________

____

____

Hop to It!

Start at 0. Count by 10s to move through the maze.

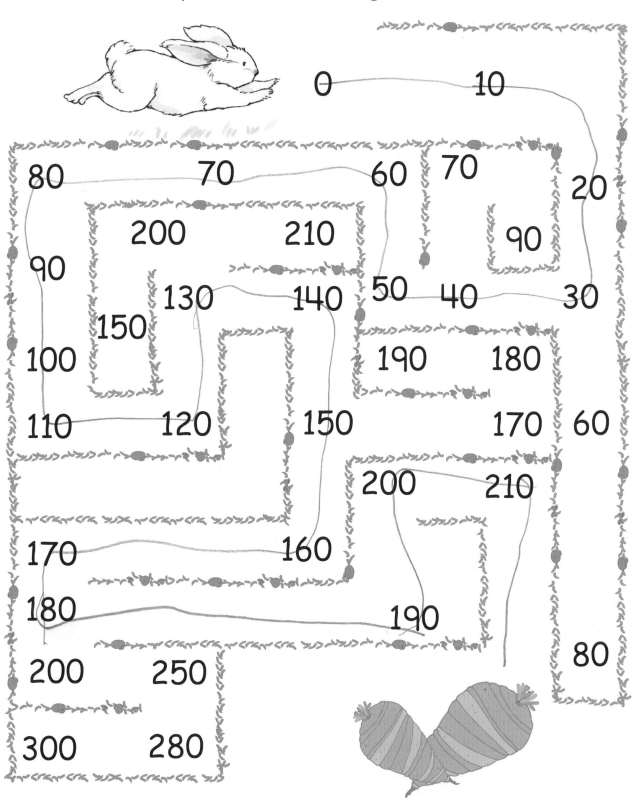

119

From A to Z

Trace the letters.

A a   B b   C c   D d   E e   F f

G g   H h   I i   J j   K k   L l

M m   N n   O o   P p   Q q   R r

S s   T t   U u   V v   W w   X x

Y y   Z z

Opposites Attract!

Cut and paste. Put the words next to their opposites.

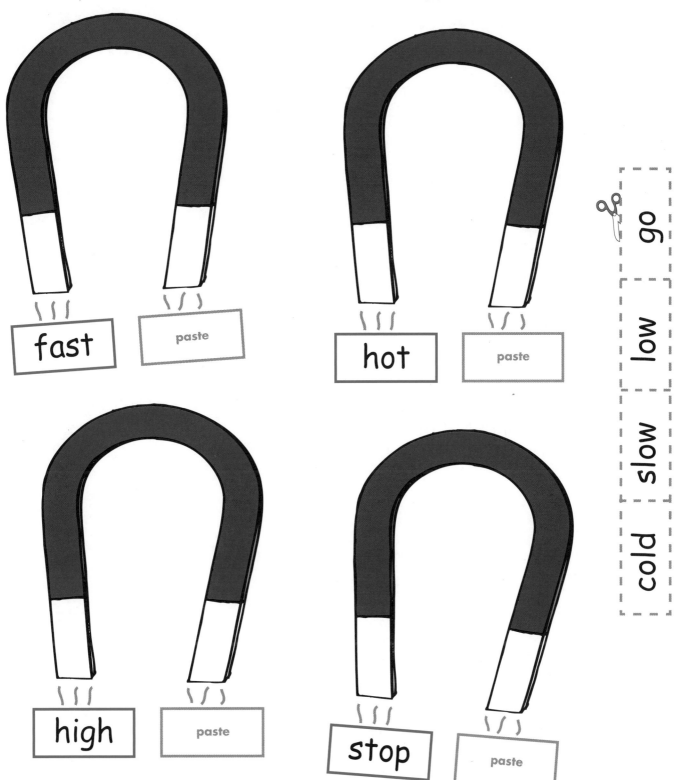

fast

paste

hot

paste

high

paste

stop

paste

go

low

slow

cold

Do You Know?

Read the rhymes. Draw a line to the
character the rhyme tells about.

Once an egg was on top of a wall.
There was a big fuss when it took a fall.

Old King Cole

She broke one important rule
When she took a sheep to school.

Jack Sprat

She was eating a snack quite content.
A guest arrived and off she went.

Miss Muffet

He only liked meat without any fat.
His wife was the opposite of that.

Little Bo-Peep

A happy gentleman was he.
He enjoyed a fiddle-dee-dee.

Humpty-Dumpty

Run, Bug, Run!

Color the words with the short u sound to help the bug run to the cupcake.

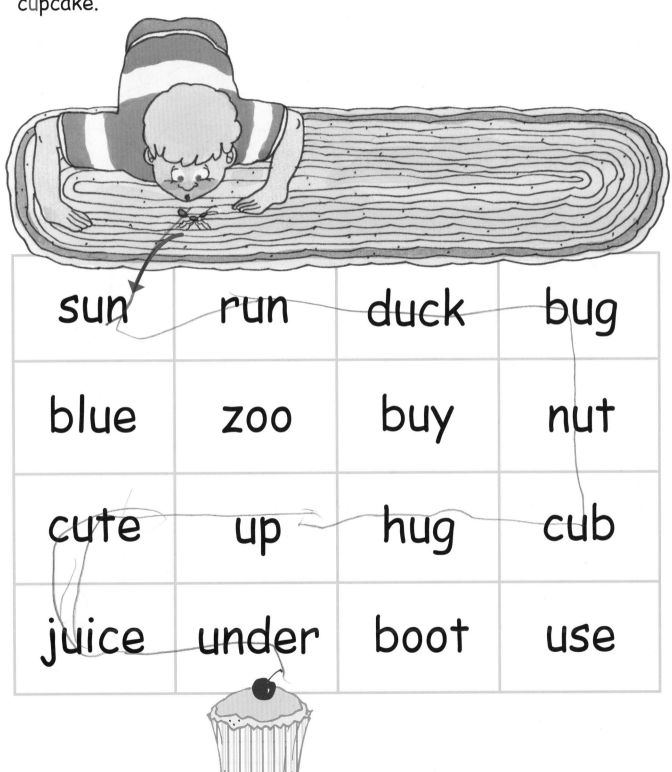

sun	run	duck	bug
blue	zoo	buy	nut
cute	up	hug	cub
juice	under	boot	use

Crazy Critter

Color the cr words.

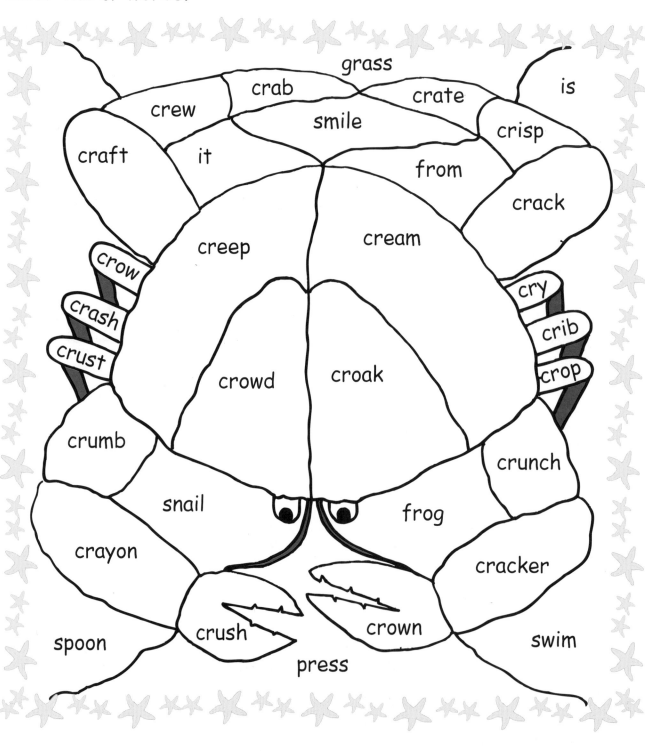

What kind of a critter did you make?_____

One Letter at a Time

Change one letter each time to make a new word.

A young dog is called a	p	u	p
A container for coffee	M	u	g
A hat for a baseball player	c	a	p
An animal that purrs	c	a	t
The opposite of thin	f	a	t
Try on shoes to see if they...	f	i	t
Do this on a chair	s	i	t
Drink slowly with a straw	___	___	___
Tilt to the side	___	___	___
A kind of metal	___	___	___
It has a sharp point	___	___	___
Something to cook in	___	___	___
A grown-up boy	___	___	___

125

Put It in Code

Use this code to write the words.

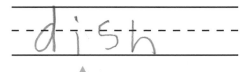

   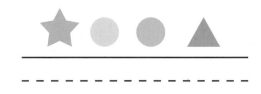

hit   dish

   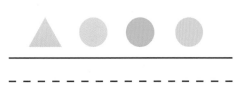

Write a word of your own in code.

A Quiet Time for Rest

Cut the pages. Make the book and read it.

staple

A Quiet Time for Rest

1

There were six in the nest
When there came a request.
Move over! Move over!
So the six moved over
and one fell out.

3

There were four in the nest
When there came a request.
Move over! Move over!
So the four moved
over and one fell out.

5

There were two in the nest
When there came a request.
Move over! Move over!
So the two moved over
and one fell out.

7

127

There were five in the nest
When there came a request.
Move over! Move over!
So the five moved
over and one fell out. 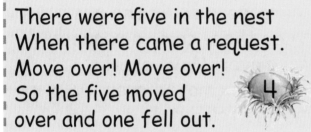 4

There were seven in the nest
When there came a request.
Move over! Move over!
So the seven moved
over and one fell out. 2

There was one in the nest
And, at last, no request.
Just a quiet time for
rest. Shhhhhhh! 8

There were three in the nest
When there came a request.
Move over! Move over!
So the three moved
over and one fell out. 6

Answer Key

Checking your child's work is an important part of learning. It allows you to see what your child knows well and what areas need more practice. It also provides an opportunity for you to help your child understand that making mistakes is a part of learning.

When an error is discovered, ask your child to look carefully at the question or problem. Errors often occur through misreading. Your child can quickly correct these errors. Help your child with items she or he finds difficult.

Page 4

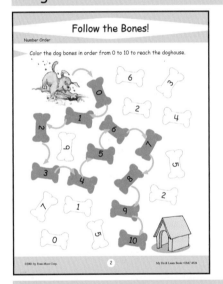

Page 5

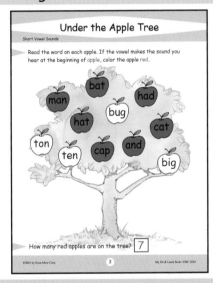

Page 6

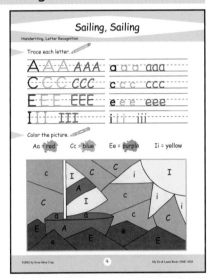

Page 7

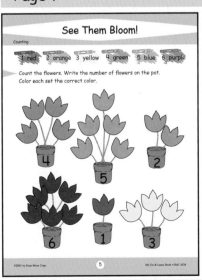

Page 8

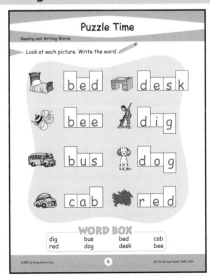

Page 9

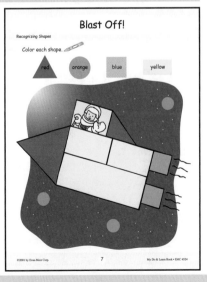

Page 10

Look Who's Cooking
Letter/Sound Association

Mark all the things that start like cup.

How many did you find? **15**

©2001 by Evan-Moor Corp.   8   My Do & Learn Book • EMC 4524

Page 11

Now I Know My ABC's
Letter Recognition, ABC Order

Connect the letters from A to Z.

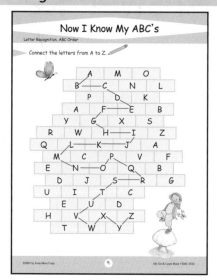

©2001 by Evan-Moor Corp.   9   My Do & Learn Book • EMC 4524

Page 12

See the Pattern
Patterning

Continue each pattern. Read the patterns.

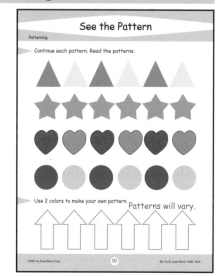

Use 2 colors to make your own pattern. **Patterns will vary.**

©2001 by Evan-Moor Corp.   10   My Do & Learn Book • EMC 4524

Page 13

An Elephant Snack
Letter/Sound Association

Use the code to crack the secret message.

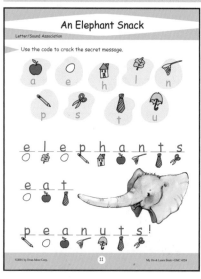

©2001 by Evan-Moor Corp.   11   My Do & Learn Book • EMC 4524

Page 14

Just Hovering!
Letter Recognition

Trace each letter.

H H H HHH   h h h hhh
J J J JJJ   j j j jjj
R R R RRR   r r r rrr

Connect the dots. Color the picture. **Picture should be colored.**

©2001 by Evan-Moor Corp.   12   My Do & Learn Book • EMC 4524

Page 15

Finish It!
Symmetry

Draw and color the missing part.

©2001 by Evan-Moor Corp.   13   My Do & Learn Book • EMC 4524

Page 16

Mind Your P's and Q's
Letter Recognition

Trace each letter.

P P P PPP   p p p ppp
Q Q Q QQQ   q q q qqq

Circle the letters that are the same.

p   p p p p q p q p
q   q p q q q p p

Follow the p's to get through the maze.

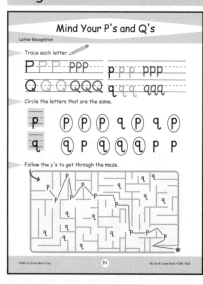

©2001 by Evan-Moor Corp.   14   My Do & Learn Book • EMC 4524

Page 17

Make a Book
Reading

Cut out the pages. Put them in order. Read the book.

One long tail,   tiny feet—

One longer tail,   Watch out, little mouse.

©2001 by Evan-Moor Corp.   15   My Do & Learn Book • EMC 4524

Page 18

This little mouse smells cheese to eat.   sharp nose,

It's a cat surprise!   two bright green eyes,

©2001 by Evan-Moor Corp.   16   My Do & Learn Book • EMC 4524

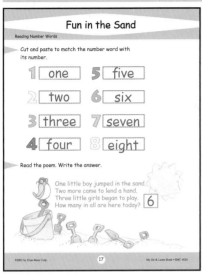

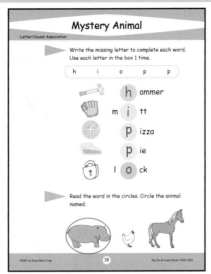

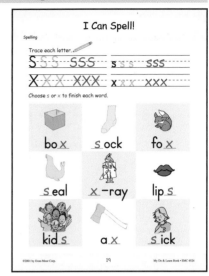

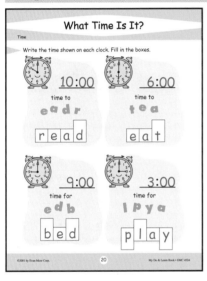

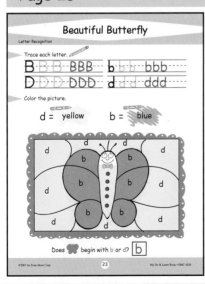

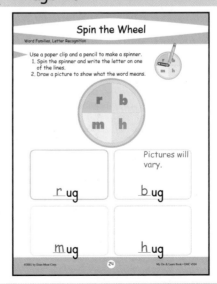

How Tall?

Measuring

The average frog jumps 20 times its height.

The frog is ___3___ blocks tall.
It can hop 60 blocks in one leap.

If you could hop like a frog, how far could you hop?

Ask an adult to help:
• Measure your height.
• Multiply by 20.

Answers will vary. That's how far you could hop!

©2001 by Evan-Moor Corp.   26   My Do & Learn Book • EMC 4524

What's Missing?

Letter/Sound Association

Write the missing letter to complete each word. Use each letter in the box 1 time.

a   e   l   p   p

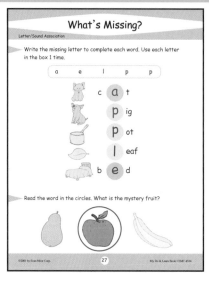

c **a** t
p ig
p ot
l eaf
b **e** d

Read the word in the circles. What is the mystery fruit?

©2001 by Evan-Moor Corp.   27   My Do & Learn Book • EMC 4524

What's Up?

Addition to 5

Solve the problems. Then connect the dots. Start with 1.

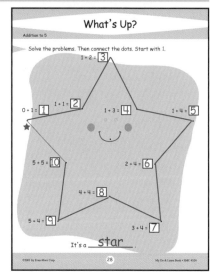

1 + 2 = 3
0 + 1 = 1   1 + 1 = 2   1 + 3 = 4   1 + 4 = 5
5 + 5 = 10   2 + 4 = 6
4 + 4 = 8
5 + 4 = 9   3 + 4 = 7

It's a ___star___

©2001 by Evan-Moor Corp.   28   My Do & Learn Book • EMC 4524

Dinner's Ready!

Categorizing

Start at the stove. Color the boxes with food words. Make a path to reach the dinner table.

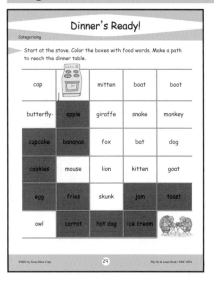

cap	mitten	boat	boot
butterfly	apple	giraffe	snake	monkey
cupcake	bananas	fox	bat	dog
cookies	mouse	lion	kitten	goat
egg	fries	skunk	jam	toast
owl	carrot	hot dog	ice cream

©2001 by Evan-Moor Corp.   29   My Do & Learn Book • EMC 4524

The Baby

Rhyming Words

Choose the correct picture. Make the poem rhyme.

Kicking feet with tiny ___toes___

Waving fists and a baby ___nose___

Soft pink cheeks and big blue ___eyes___

First he coos and then he ___cries___

©2001 by Evan-Moor Corp.   30   My Do & Learn Book • EMC 4524

At the Circus

Alphabet Recognition

Connect the dots to discover the circus animal. Start with A. Color the picture.

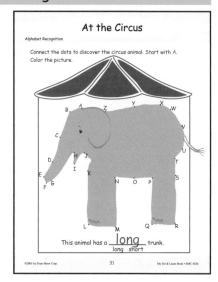

This animal has a ___long___ trunk.
long   short

©2001 by Evan-Moor Corp.   31   My Do & Learn Book • EMC 4524

Picking Up Pennies!

Money

Help Peter get to the Popcorn Palace. Follow the pennies. Each time he passes a penny in the path, Peter picks it up and puts it in his pouch. When he gets to the Popcorn Palace, help him decide what to buy.

What will Peter buy? Make sure that he has enough money for the thing or things you choose.

10¢   or   7¢   15¢

©2001 by Evan-Moor Corp.   32   My Do & Learn Book • EMC 4524

A Rainbow of Hats

Color Words

Unscramble each color word. Color the hats.

red   orange   yellow   green
blue   purple   pink   brown

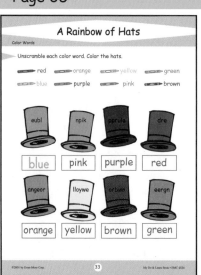

eubl → blue   npik → pink   pprula → purple   dre → red

angeor → orange   lloywe → yellow   orbwn → brown   eergn → green

©2001 by Evan-Moor Corp.   33   My Do & Learn Book • EMC 4524

Change the Story

Antonyms

Read ①.
Replace each green word with its opposite in ②.
Read ②.

① The little boy went up the ladder.
He stopped at the top.
He looked down.
Then he waved hello.

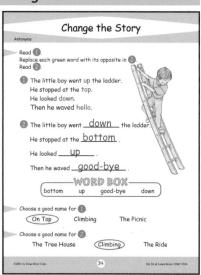

② The little boy went ___down___ the ladder.
He stopped at the ___bottom___.
He looked ___up___.
Then he waved ___good-bye___.

WORD BOX
bottom   up   good-bye   down

Choose a good name for ①
(On Top)   Climbing   The Picnic

Choose a good name for ②
The Tree House   (Climbing)   The Ride

©2001 by Evan-Moor Corp.   34   My Do & Learn Book • EMC 4524

Page 37

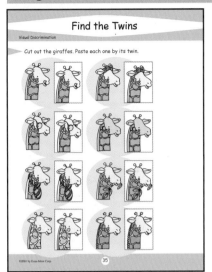

Find the Twins

Visual Discrimination

Cut out the giraffes. Paste each one by its twin.

Page 38

Page 39

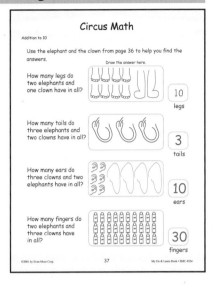

Circus Math

Addition to 10

Use the elephant and the clown from page 36 to help you find the answers.

How many legs do two elephants and one clown have in all? — **10** legs

How many tails do three elephants and two clowns have in all? — **3** tails

How many ears do three clowns and two elephants have in all? — **10** ears

How many fingers do two elephants and three clowns have in all? — **30** fingers

Page 40

Lines and Circles

Handwriting

Trace each letter.

K K K KKK k k k kkk
L L L LLL l l l lll
E E E EEE e e e eee
Y Y Y YYY y y y yyy
Z Z Z ZZZ z z z zzz
O O O OOO o o o ooo

Write the answers to the questions.

How can you find something that is lost using only your eyes? — **look**

Where can you find a roaring lion and a snoring hippo? — **zoo**

What can you do at the ball game but not at the library? — **yell**

WORD BOX
zoo   yell   look

Page 41

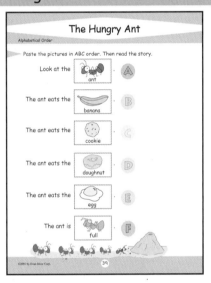

The Hungry Ant

Alphabetical Order

Paste the pictures in ABC order. Then read the story.

Look at the — ant — A
The ant eats the — banana — B
The ant eats the — cookie — C
The ant eats the — doughnut — D
The ant eats the — egg — E
The ant is — full — F

Page 42

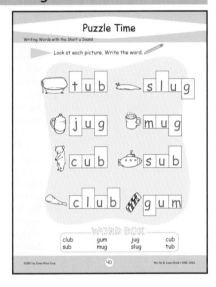

Puzzle Time

Writing Words with the Short u Sound

Look at each picture. Write the word.

tub   slug
jug   mug
cub   sub
club   gum

WORD BOX
club   gum   jug   cub
sub   mug   slug   tub

Page 43

A Snowy Day

Categorizing

Mark the things Carlos should wear to build a snowman.

Page 44

Ready for Fun!

Reading Comprehension

Read the sentences. Add the things to the picture.

I have one green hat.

I have two purple bags.

I have three orange flowers.

I have four purple balloons.

I have five blue pockets.

I have one red lollipop in each pocket.

I'm ready for fun!

Page 45

On My Street

Addition to 5

Solve each math problem. Color the picture.

Page 46

A Riddle

Subtraction to 6

Solve each math problem. Use the code to answer the riddle. Write the letter that goes with each answer on the line.

a	e	n	p	r	s	w
0	1	2	3	4	5	6

What is black and white and read all over?

$\frac{1}{-1}$	$\frac{2}{-0}$	$\frac{4}{-3}$	$\frac{6}{-0}$	$\frac{6}{-1}$
0 a	2 n	1 e	6 w	5 s

$\frac{4}{-1}$	$\frac{3}{-3}$	$\frac{5}{-2}$	$\frac{2}{-1}$	$\frac{4}{-0}$
3 p	0 a	3 p	1 e	4 r

Answer:

a newspaper

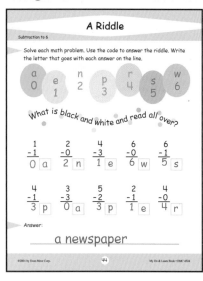

Page 47

A Word Search

Visual Discrimination

Find the words and circle them.

```
H A M B U R G E R E P S
Z E B R A P J M C T P Q
R U D O W X P S B R Z I
O H C O W E C W W T E I
C B P E A S Q V O L K H
M N D I T R E E I P Y
W S H Y D B U N N Y B W
A L L I G A T O R R I C
N F H X O Z C G R A S S
M J M U N F L O W E R J
R N P K A S C Q W M T M
G R A P E S J U O J Y Q
```

WORD BOX

alligator	cow	flower	grapes	grass
hamburger	peas	tree	zebra	bunny

Page 48

Under the Sea

Subtraction

Solve each problem. Use the color key to color the picture.

green = 0   orange = 1   yellow = 2   blue = 3

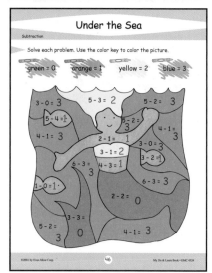

Page 49

Riding a Bike

Reading Comprehension

Cut the pages. Make the book. Read the story.

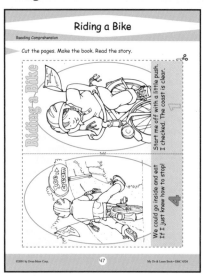

Page 50

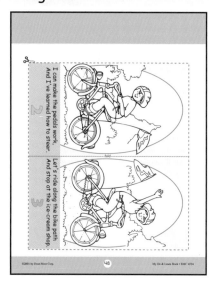

Page 51

Follow the Balloons

Recognizing Words with the Short e Sound

Color the balloons that have the short e sound like you hear in [hen].

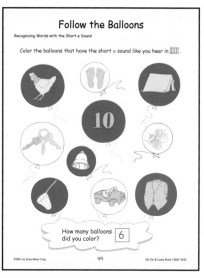

How many balloons did you color? 6

Page 52

Here Kitty, Kitty

Reading Sight Words

Read each sentence. Draw Kitty in each picture.

Kitty is on the bed.

Kitty is up the tree.

Kitty is under the desk.

Kitty is in the tub.

Page 53

How Many Spots?

Number Sense

In each circle, count the number of spots on Dog 1 and write the number. Draw 1 less spot on Dog 2 and write the number.

Dog 1   Dog 2   Dog 1   Dog 2
3   2   6   5

Dog 1   Dog 2   Dog 1   Dog 2
2   1   5   4

Page 54

Happy Day

Counting and Number Words

Count the smiles. Write the number word in the puzzle.

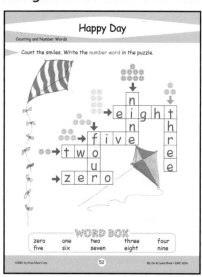

WORD BOX

zero	one	two	three	four
five	six	seven	eight	nine

Koala Puppet

Reading Comprehension

Cut out this koala puppet and ears. Fold on the line. Paste the edge closed. Paste on the ears.

Koalas live in special trees. Eucalyptus! They like to eat the tasty leaves.

Put Koala on your hand. Tell about their home in Australia.

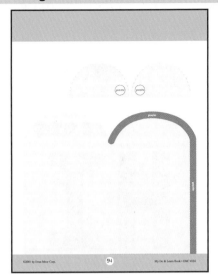

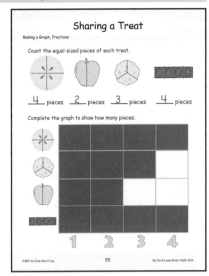

Sharing a Treat

Making a Graph, Fractions

Count the equal-sized pieces of each treat.

4 pieces   2 pieces   3 pieces   4 pieces

Complete the graph to show how many pieces.

1   2   3   4

Lots of Colors

Color Words

Write the name of the color in each box.

WORD BOX
black   blue   brown   gray   green   orange
pink   purple   red   white   yellow

A Celebration

Comprehension

Cut the pages. Make a little book. Read the story.

A Celebration

Sticks and mud
and dry, brown grass
Make a robin's nest first class!

Three tiny sky blue eggs
Tucked underneath her legs.

Mother Robin sits and waits.
Then, of course, she celebrates.

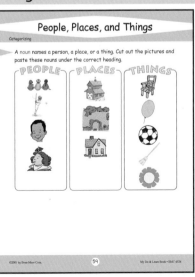

People, Places, and Things

Categorizing

A noun names a person, a place, or a thing. Cut out the pictures and paste these nouns under the correct heading.

PEOPLE   PLACES   THINGS

What Colors Do You See?

Color Words

Find each word.

X P U R P L E A B T
G R E E N B R O W N
R E D S Y E L L O W
B L A C K G R A Y U
B L U E O R A N G E
W H I T E N P I N K

WORD BOX
black   blue   brown   gray   green   orange
pink   purple   red   white   yellow

Parents and Babies

Vocabulary

Cut and paste. Match each parent with its baby.

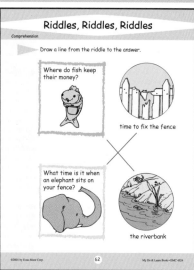

Riddles, Riddles, Riddles

Comprehension

Draw a line from the riddle to the answer.

Where do fish keep their money?

time to fix the fence

What time is it when an elephant sits on your fence?

the riverbank

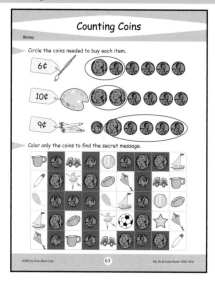

Counting Coins

Money

Circle the coins needed to buy each item.

6¢   10¢   9¢

Color only the coins to find the secret message.

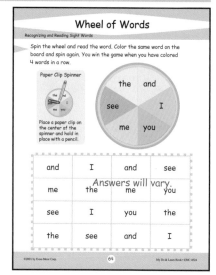

Wheel of Words

Recognizing and Reading Sight Words

Spin the wheel and read the word. Color the same word on the board and spin again. You win the game when you have colored 4 words in a row.

Paper Clip Spinner

the   and
see   I
me   you

Place a paper clip on the center of the spinner and hold in place with a pencil.

and	I	and	see
me	the	me	you
see	I	you	the
the	see	and	I

Answers will vary.

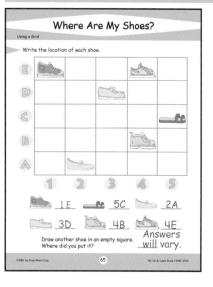

Where Are My Shoes?

Using a Grid

Write the location of each shoe.

1E   5C   2A
3D   4B   4E

Draw another shoe in an empty square. Where did you put it?
Answers will vary.

Dandy Dinosaurs

Reading a Chart

Use the information on the chart to answer the questions.

Brachiosaurus   Triceratops   Stegosaurus   Tyrannosaurus Rex

Which dinosaur is shorter?

Which dinosaur is 15 feet tall?

How tall is Triceratops?   10 feet

Which dinosaur is taller than Tyrannosaurus Rex?   Brachiosaurus

Friends Come in Many Sizes

Reading Words

Cut the pages. Make the book. Read the story.

Friends Come in Many Sizes

Friends can be tall or short. Their size doesn't matter.

Friends can be old or young. Their age doesn't matter.

Fast or slow, tall or short, loud or quiet, old or young, near or far away—the important thing about friends is that they care about you and you care about them.

Friends can be loud or quiet. Their volume doesn't matter.

Friends can be fast or slow. Their speed doesn't matter.

Draw a picture of some of your friends.

Friends can be near or far away. Where they are doesn't matter.

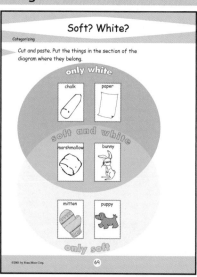

Soft? White?

Categorizing

Cut and paste. Put the things in the section of the diagram where they belong.

only white
chalk   paper

soft and white
marshmallow   bunny

mitten   puppy

only soft

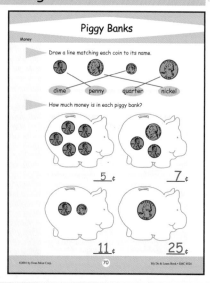

Piggy Banks

Money

Draw a line matching each coin to its name.

dime   penny   quarter   nickel

How much money is in each piggy bank?

5 ¢   7 ¢

11 ¢   25 ¢

A Scrambled Sentence

Sentence Order and Reading Sight Words

Cut and paste the words to make a sentence. Color the picture.

| The | little | bird | slept |
| in | his | cozy | bed. |

©2001 by Evan-Moor Corp. 71

Big Bears and Little Bears

Following Directions

Draw a big bear. Draw several little bears.

©2001 by Evan-Moor Corp. 72

Taking Care of Your Body

Reading Comprehension

Cut the pages. Make the book. Read the story.

©2001 by Evan-Moor Corp. 73 My Do & Learn Book • EMC 4524

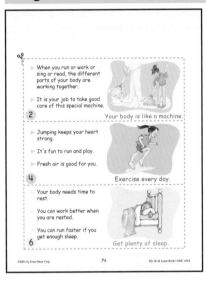

©2001 by Evan-Moor Corp. 74 My Do & Learn Book • EMC 4524

Naming Patterns

Labeling Patterns

Finish labeling each pattern.

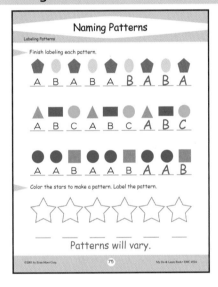

A B A B A B A B A

A B C A B C A B C

A A B A A B A A B

Color the stars to make a pattern. Label the pattern.

Patterns will vary.

©2001 by Evan-Moor Corp. 75 My Do & Learn Book • EMC 4524

Saying the Same Thing

Synonyms

Synonyms are different words with the same meanings. Look at each picture. Circle the two words with the same meaning that go with the picture.

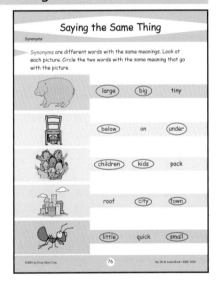

large big tiny

below on under

children kids pack

roof city town

little quick small

©2001 by Evan-Moor Corp. 76 My Do & Learn Book • EMC 4524

A Secret Message

Letter/Sound Association

Write the missing letter for each word. Then write the letter on the line with the same number.

1. f_an 2. p_in 3. S_and 4. h_ug

5. C_andy 6. a_pple 7. gree_n 8. S_un

9. W_agon 10. h_i_ppo 11. le_m_on

Read the secret message.

f i s h   c a n
1 2 3 4   5 6 7

s w i m
8 9 10 11

©2001 by Evan-Moor Corp. 77 My Do & Learn Book • EMC 4524

First or Last?

Handwriting, Letter/Sound Association

Trace the letters.

F F F FFF f f f fff
T T T TTT t t t ttt

Name the pictures. Color the squares.

t at the end—red
t at the beginning—green
f at the end—yellow
f at the beginning—purple

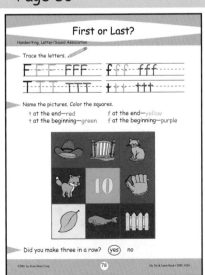

Did you make three in a row? yes no

©2001 by Evan-Moor Corp. 78 My Do & Learn Book • EMC 4524

Two Scoops

Contractions

Cut out the scoops of ice cream. Glue the 2 scoops to show the words that make the contraction on each ice-cream cone.

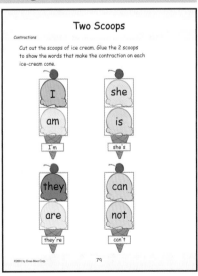

I / am — I'm
she / is — she's
they / are — they're
can / not — can't

©2001 by Evan-Moor Corp. 79

Mr. Smiles
Alphabetical Order

▶ Connect the dots. Start with A. Color the picture.

©2001 by Evan-Moor Corp. • 80 • My Do & Learn Book • EMC 4524

We Salute You
Addition to 10

▶ Add. Color each box.

7 = black   8 = red   9 = white   10 = blue

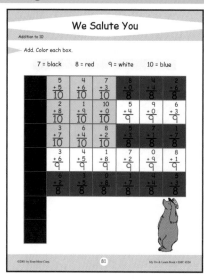

©2001 by Evan-Moor Corp. • 81 • My Do & Learn Book • EMC 4524

Places to Go
Reading Words

▶ Complete the crossword puzzle.

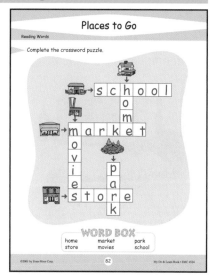

WORD BOX

home	market	park
store	movies	school

©2001 by Evan-Moor Corp. • 82 • My Do & Learn Book • EMC 4524

A Riddle
Letter/Sound Association

▶ Read the riddle. Write the beginning letter of each picture to decode the answer.

Why was Cinderella thrown off the baseball team?

Because she ran away from the ball

©2001 by Evan-Moor Corp. • 83 • My Do & Learn Book • EMC 4524

Who Lives Here?
Subtraction

▶ Subtract. Color the picture.

6 brown   5 blue   7 orange

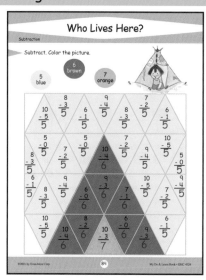

©2001 by Evan-Moor Corp. • 84 • My Do & Learn Book • EMC 4524

Surprise!
Using Punctuation Marks

▶ Read the story. Complete each sentence using the correct punctuation mark.

We went to the park	.	period
It is Jon's birthday	.	exclamation point
Happy Birthday, Jon	!	question mark
Do you see a surprise	?
It is a surprise for Jon	.
If you do, yell, "SURPRISE"	!

Color the picture to see what the surprise is.

. = red
! = blue
? = yellow

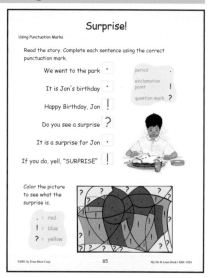

©2001 by Evan-Moor Corp. • 85 • My Do & Learn Book • EMC 4524

In the Ocean
Visual Discrimination

▶ Find the words in the word search.

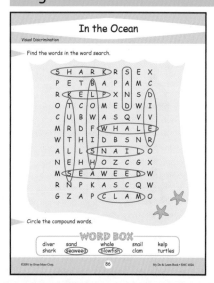

▶ Circle the compound words.

WORD BOX

diver	sand	whale	snail	kelp
shark	seaweed	blowfish	clam	turtles

©2001 by Evan-Moor Corp. • 86 • My Do & Learn Book • EMC 4524

Gone Camping
Measuring

▶ Cut out the centimeter ruler and measure each piece of camping equipment.

The lantern is 7 cm tall.
The fishing pole is 8 cm long.
The sign is 9 cm tall.
The tent is 7 cm long.
The canoe is 13 cm long.

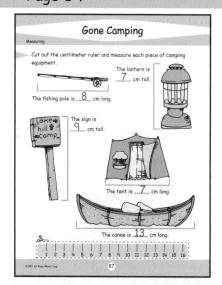

©2001 by Evan-Moor Corp. • 87 • My Do & Learn Book • EMC 4524

7 Days
Days of the Week

▶ Decode each day of the week. Number the days to put them in order. Start with Sunday.

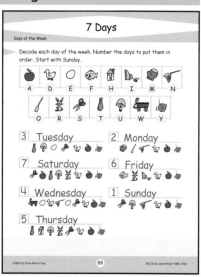

3 Tuesday   2 Monday
7 Saturday   6 Friday
4 Wednesday   1 Sunday
5 Thursday

©2001 by Evan-Moor Corp. • 88 • My Do & Learn Book • EMC 4524

Page 91

A Full Year

Visual Discrimination

Find each month's name in the word search.

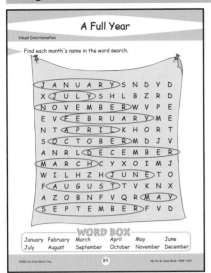

WORD BOX

January	February	March	April	May	June
July	August	September	October	November	December

©2001 by Evan-Moor Corp. 89 My Do & Learn Book • EMC 4524

Page 92

The Mystery Shape

Geometric Shapes

Make an X on any shape that fits the clues. The mystery shape will be left.

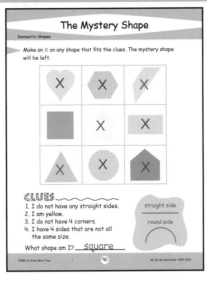

CLUES

1. I do not have any straight sides.
2. I am yellow.
3. I do not have 4 corners.
4. I have 4 sides that are not all the same size.

What shape am I? square

straight side
round side

©2001 by Evan-Moor Corp. 90 My Do & Learn Book • EMC 4524

Page 93

Begins with G

Letter Recognition

Trace each letter.

G G G GGG   g g g ggg

Cut and paste. Put the puzzle together.
How many things in the picture begin with a g? 3

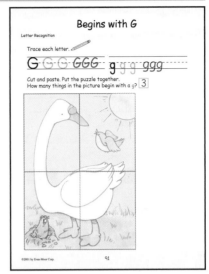

©2001 by Evan-Moor Corp. 91

Page 94

Interesting Insects

Comprehension

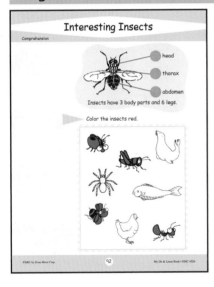

head
thorax
abdomen

Insects have 3 body parts and 6 legs.

Color the insects red.

©2001 by Evan-Moor Corp. 92 My Do & Learn Book • EMC 4524

Page 95

Contraction Caterpillars

Contractions

Cut and paste. Fill each caterpillar with the two words that make its contractions.

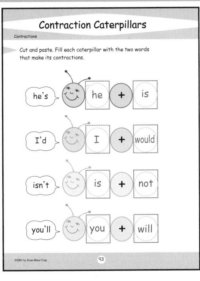

he's   he + is
I'd   I + would
isn't   is + not
you'll you + will

©2001 by Evan-Moor Corp. 93

Page 96

I Love Pancakes

Comprehension

Sing this pancake song. (Sung to the tune of "Brother John")

I love pancakes.
I love pancakes.
Yes I do.
Yes I do.

I can eat them everyday.
I can eat them anyway.
Yes, I can.
Yes, I can.

Number the pictures in order.

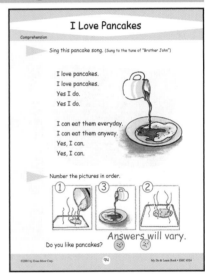

1   3   2

Do you like pancakes?

Answers will vary.

©2001 by Evan-Moor Corp. 94 My Do & Learn Book • EMC 4524

Page 97

Riddle Me a Shape

Recognizing Shapes

Draw the shape that answers each riddle.

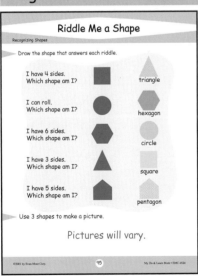

I have 4 sides.
Which shape am I?   triangle

I can roll.
Which shape am I?   hexagon

I have 6 sides.
Which shape am I?   circle

I have 3 sides.
Which shape am I?   square

I have 5 sides.
Which shape am I?   pentagon

Use 3 shapes to make a picture.

Pictures will vary.

©2001 by Evan-Moor Corp. 95 My Do & Learn Book • EMC 4524

Page 98

Be a Letter Detective

Letter Recognition

Trace each letter.

M M M MM   m m m mmm
N N NNN   n n nnn
U U U UUU   u u uuu
W W WW   w w www

Some lowercase letters are similar. Color the squares to show you can read these letters:

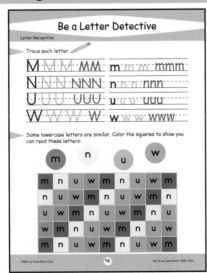

m   n   u   w

m	n	u	w	m	n	u	w
n	u	w	m	n	u	w	m
u	w	m	n	u	w	m	n
w	m	n	u	w	m	n	u
m	n	u	w	m	n	u	w

©2001 by Evan-Moor Corp. 96 My Do & Learn Book • EMC 4524

Page 99

Which One Is First?

Alphabetical Order

Cut out the pictures. Glue them in alphabetical order.

A B C D E F G H I J K L M
N O P Q R S T U V W X Y Z

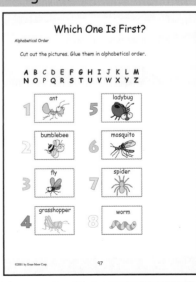

1 ant   5 ladybug
2 bumblebee   6 mosquito
3 fly   7 spider
4 grasshopper 8 worm

©2001 by Evan-Moor Corp. 97

Page 100

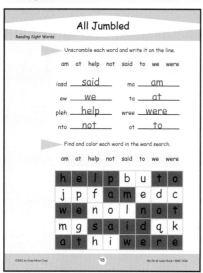

All Jumbled

Reading Sight Words

▶ Unscramble each word and write it on the line.

am at help not said to we were

iasd **said**　　　ma **am**

ew **we**　　　ta **at**

pleh **help**　　　wree **were**

nto **not**　　　ot **to**

▶ Find and color each word in the word search.

am at help not said to we were

h	e	l	p	b	u	t	o
j	p	f	a	m	e	d	c
w	e	n	o	l	n	o	t
m	g	s	a	i	d	q	k
a	t	h	i	w	e	r	e

©2001 by Evan-Moor Corp.　98　My Do & Learn Book • EMC 4524

Page 101

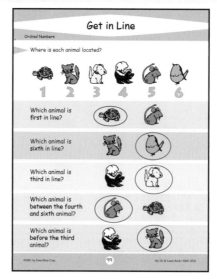

Get in Line

Ordinal Numbers

▶ Where is each animal located?

1 2 3 4 5 6

Which animal is first in line?

Which animal is sixth in line?

Which animal is third in line?

Which animal is between the fourth and sixth animal?

Which animal is before the third animal?

©2001 by Evan-Moor Corp.　99　My Do & Learn Book • EMC 4524

Page 102

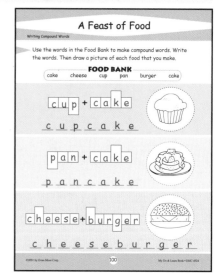

A Feast of Food

Writing Compound Words

▶ Use the words in the Food Bank to make compound words. Write the words. Then draw a picture of each food that you make.

FOOD BANK

cake cheese cup pan burger cake

cup + cake

c u p c a k e

pan + cake

p a n c a k e

cheese + burger

c h e e s e b u r g e r

©2001 by Evan-Moor Corp.　100　My Do & Learn Book • EMC 4524

Page 103

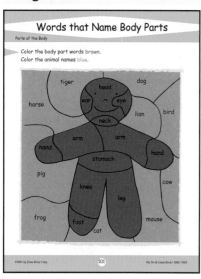

Words that Name Body Parts

Parts of the Body

▶ Color the body part words brown.
Color the animal names blue.

tiger dog head eye ear horse lion bird neck arm arm hand stomach hand pig cow knee leg frog foot cat mouse

©2001 by Evan-Moor Corp.　101　My Do & Learn Book • EMC 4524

Page 104

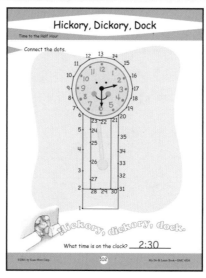

Hickory, Dickory, Dock

Time to the Half Hour

▶ Connect the dots.

Hickory, dickory, dock.

What time is on the clock? **2:30**

©2001 by Evan-Moor Corp.　102　My Do & Learn Book • EMC 4524

Page 105

A Sleepover

Reading

Cut the pages. Make the book.

A Sleepover

I'm packing up my suitcase.
Tori invited me next door.
We're going to have fun.
I'll put in a few things more.

I'm packing up my suitcase.
I'm going by myself, you see.
My family will stay home.
Tori called and asked just me.

I'm packing up my suitcase.
I just can't wait to go.
A sleepover is the very most
Exciting thing I know!

©2001 by Evan-Moor Corp.　103　My Do & Learn Book • EMC 4524

Page 106

I'm packing up my suitcase
For a sleepover—my very first!
I'm getting so excited,
I think that I might burst!

I'm packing up my suitcase.
I'll put in all my stuff.
I'm taking an important trip.
I hope I brought enough.

Answers will vary.

Make a list of things you would take on a sleepover.

I'm packing up my suitcase.
I made a list of things to bring.
You never know when you might
Just forget to pack something.

©2001 by Evan-Moor Corp.　104　My Do & Learn Book • EMC 4524

Page 107

Find the Question

Letter Recognition

▶ Color the boxes with d red. Color the boxes with b blue.
Color the boxes with p green. Color the boxes with q yellow.

January February March April May June July August September October November December

p	h	o	w	d	b	m	a	n	y
q	d	m	o	n	t	h	s	p	b
a	r	e	d	q	b	p	i	n	d
q	b	a	p	d	y	e	a	r	?

▶ Read the white boxes. Answer the question.

12 months

©2001 by Evan-Moor Corp.　105　My Do & Learn Book • EMC 4524

Page 108

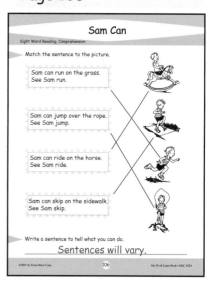

Sam Can

Sight Word Reading, Comprehension

▶ Match the sentence to the picture.

Sam can run on the grass.
See Sam run.

Sam can jump over the rope.
See Sam jump.

Sam can ride on the horse.
See Sam ride.

Sam can skip on the sidewalk.
See Sam skip.

▶ Write a sentence to tell what you can do.

Sentences will vary.

©2001 by Evan-Moor Corp.　106　My Do & Learn Book • EMC 4524

Page 109

On Your Mark, Get Set, Go!

Counting by 2s

Find your way to the finish line by coloring the numbers used when counting by 2s.

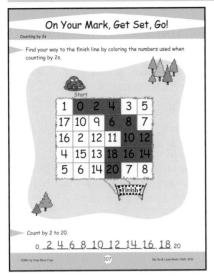

Count by 2 to 20.

0, _2_ _4_ _6_ _8_ _10_ _12_ _14_ _16_ _18_, 20

©2001 by Evan-Moor Corp.   107   My Do & Learn Book • EMC 4524

Page 110

Stop-Go, Yes-No

Antonyms

Label each picture. Draw lines to connect the opposites.

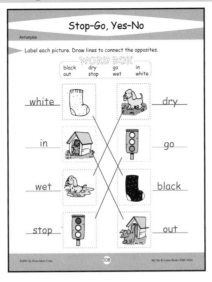

WORD BOX
black dry go in
out stop wet white

white — dry
in — go
wet — black
stop — out

©2001 by Evan-Moor Corp.   108   My Do & Learn Book • EMC 4524

Page 111

Counting by Fives

Counting by 5s

Complete the pattern by counting by 5s.

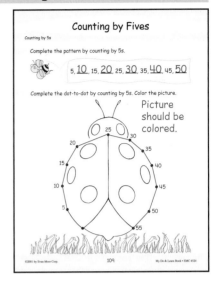

5, _10_, 15, _20_, 25, _30_, 35, _40_, 45, _50_

Complete the dot-to-dot by counting by 5s. Color the picture.

Picture should be colored.

©2001 by Evan-Moor Corp.   109   My Do & Learn Book • EMC 4524

Page 112

Hop Along, Froggy

Rhyming Words

Circle the lily pads that have two words that rhyme.

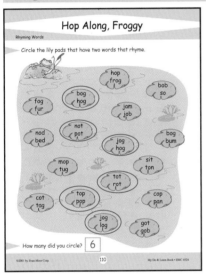

How many did you circle? 6

©2001 by Evan-Moor Corp.   110   My Do & Learn Book • EMC 4524

Page 113

Tic Tac Toe

Short o Sound

Draw a line matching each picture with its name.

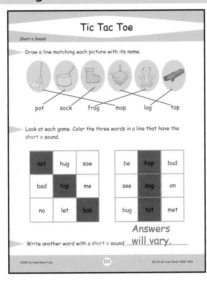

pot sock frog mop log top

Look at each game. Color the three words in a line that have the short o sound.

not	hug	saw
bad	top	me
no	let	bob

be	hop	bud
see	dog	on
bug	tot	met

Write another word with a short o sound.   Answers will vary.

©2001 by Evan-Moor Corp.   111   My Do & Learn Book • EMC 4524

Page 114

A Hundreds Chart

Counting by 10s

Write the missing numbers. Color all the squares with a 3 red. Color all the squares with a 2 blue. Color all the squares with a 4 yellow.

Which squares did you color twice?
23, 24, 32, 34, 42, 43

Did they change color?
yes no

Color the rest of the squares. Make your own pattern.

©2001 by Evan-Moor Corp.   112   My Do & Learn Book • EMC 4524

Page 115

Fun with Pennies

Addition with Pennies

Cut and paste. Give each person 5¢.

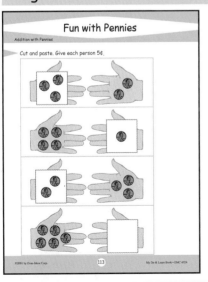

©2001 by Evan-Moor Corp.   113   My Do & Learn Book • EMC 4524

Page 116

Big and Little

Letter Recognition

Circle each pair of capital and lowercase letters.

ABCDEFGHIJKLMNOPQRSTUVWXYZ

Write the lowercase letter.

A a   C c   T t   M m

Write the capital letter

g G   b B   u U   s S

©2001 by Evan-Moor Corp.   114   My Do & Learn Book • EMC 4524

Page 117

Words with Long e

Long e Sound

Draw a line through the long e words in each puzzle.

long e sound as in feet

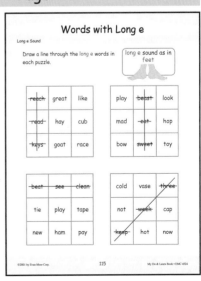

~~reach~~	great	like
~~read~~	hay	cub
~~keys~~	goat	race

play	~~beast~~	look
mad	~~eat~~	hop
bow	~~sweet~~	toy

~~beat~~	~~see~~	~~clean~~
tie	play	tape
new	ham	pay

cold	vase	~~three~~
not	~~week~~	cap
~~keep~~	hot	now

©2001 by Evan-Moor Corp.   115   My Do & Learn Book • EMC 4524

Page 118

Change It!

Reading

Choose one from each box. Write a sentence. Draw a picture to show what your sentence means.

Baby	ate	a cookie.
Dad	chopped	some weeds.
Mom	washed	the dirty dishes.
Grandpa	painted	the gate.

1. Sentences and pictures will vary.

2.

3.

©2001 by Evan-Moor Corp.   116   My Do & Learn Book • EMC 4524

Page 119

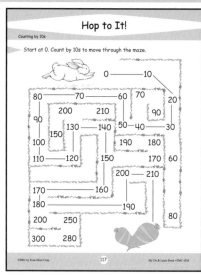

Hop to It!

Counting by 10s

Start at 0. Count by 10s to move through the maze.

©2001 by Evan-Moor Corp.   117   My Do & Learn Book • EMC 4524

Page 120

From A to Z

Handwriting

Trace the letters.

Aa Bb Cc Dd Ee Ff
Gg Hh Ii Jj Kk Ll
Mm Nn Oo Pp Qq Rr
Ss Tt Uu Vv Ww Xx
Yy Zz

©2001 by Evan-Moor Corp.   118   My Do & Learn Book • EMC 4524

Page 121

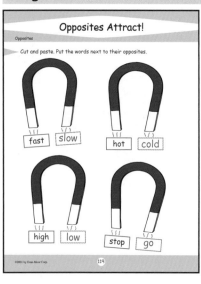

Opposites Attract!

Opposites

Cut and paste. Put the words next to their opposites.

fast — slow
hot — cold
high — low
stop — go

©2001 by Evan-Moor Corp.   119   My Do & Learn Book • EMC 4524

Page 122

Do You Know?

Making Inferences

Read the rhymes. Draw a line to the character the rhyme tells about.

Once an egg was on top of a wall.
There was a big fuss when it took a fall.

She broke one important rule
When she took a sheep to school.

She was eating a snack quite content.
A guest arrived and off she went.

He only liked meat without any fat.
His wife was the opposite of that.

A happy gentleman was he.
He enjoyed a fiddle-dee-dee.

Old King Cole
Jack Sprat
Miss Muffet
Little Bo-Peep
Humpty-Dumpty

©2001 by Evan-Moor Corp.   120   My Do & Learn Book • EMC 4524

Page 123

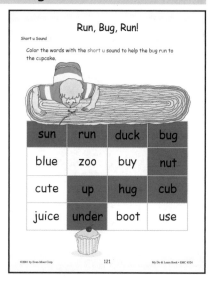

Run, Bug, Run!

Short u Sound

Color the words with the short u sound to help the bug run to the cupcake.

sun	run	duck	bug
blue	zoo	buy	nut
cute	up	hug	cub
juice	under	boot	use

©2001 by Evan-Moor Corp.   121   My Do & Learn Book • EMC 4524

Page 124

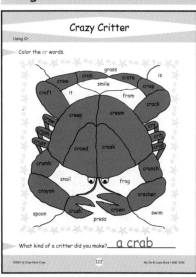

Crazy Critter

Using Cr

Color the cr words.

What kind of a critter did you make? a crab

©2001 by Evan-Moor Corp.   122   My Do & Learn Book • EMC 4524

Page 125

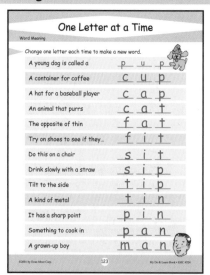

One Letter at a Time

Word Meaning

Change one letter each time to make a new word.

A young dog is called a	p u p
A container for coffee	c u p
A hat for a baseball player	c a p
An animal that purrs	c a t
The opposite of thin	f a t
Try on shoes to see if they…	f i t
Do this on a chair	s i t
Drink slowly with a straw	s i p
Tilt to the side	t i p
A kind of metal	t i n
It has a sharp point	p i n
Something to cook in	p a n
A grown-up boy	m a n

©2001 by Evan-Moor Corp.   123   My Do & Learn Book • EMC 4524

Page 126

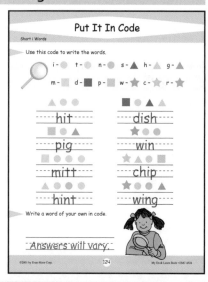

Put It In Code

Short i Words

Use this code to write the words.

i - ● t - ● n - ● s - ▲ h - ▲ g - ▲
m - ■ d - ■ p - ■ w - ★ c - ★ r - ★

hit   dish
pig   win
mitt   chip
hint   wing

Write a word of your own in code.

Answers will vary.

©2001 by Evan-Moor Corp.   124   My Do & Learn Book • EMC 4524

Good-bye

I'm done.
I'm done.
I'm done.

So long.
So long.
A farewell song.

Good-bye.
Good-bye.
Please don't cry.

Adieu.
Adieu.
From me to you.

EMC 6309 • © Evan-Moor Corp.

The Never-Bored Kid Book 2